MR. MACREADY PRODUCES

AS YOU LIKE IT

=

as you like it   Nº 11

Jaques

MR. MACREADY AS JAQUES
The costume design by Charles Hamilton Smith.

MR. MACREADY PRODUCES

AS YOU LIKE IT;

A PROMPT-BOOK STUDY

Charles H. Shattuck

———

Beta Phi Mu

1962

Beta Phi Mu Chapbook Number Five/Six

Urbana, Illinois

Library of Congress Catalog Card Number 62-21425

PRINTED IN GREAT BRITAIN BY W. S. COWELL LTD
AT THE BUTTER MARKET, IPSWICH, ENGLAND

PREFACE

When the first of these chapbooks was published in 1953, Beta Phi Mu was only four years old. Its membership consisted of honor graduates of the University of Illinois Library School who were interested in sponsoring professional and scholarly projects pertaining to their profession. The organization proposed in addition to further the art of book design by issuing a series of publications in which the designer would be given complete freedom to experiment.

Since the appearance of Chapbook Number One, Beta Phi Mu has become not only national in scope but international; its Delta chapter was established in London in 1957. It is fitting therefore that this latest chapbook, *Mr. Macready Produces "As You Like It,"* was designed and manufactured in England. The designer was Maurice Walker of W. S. Cowell Ltd whose Design Director is John Lewis, F.S.I.A., lecturer at the Royal College of Art.

The editor, Charles H. Shattuck, has long been interested in theatre history and play direction, pursuits which led to his studies of prompt-books. His enthusiasm for Macready's *As You Like It* convinced Beta Phi Mu's publications committee that it should be added to the Chapbook series. Shortly after decision was made to publish, Professor Shattuck received a Guggenheim Foundation award to continue his investigations into prompt-books —an occurrence which may indicate that the Chapbook series is alert for important trends.

Because of its size and the expense of printing, this chapbook carries a double number, 5/6. Publication would not have been possible without the aid of Ernest Ingold of San Francisco. Mr. Ingold presented the original prompt-book to the University of Illinois Library, and when he learned of Beta Phi Mu's interest in reproducing it, he generously assisted with publication costs.

The publications committee would also like to express thanks to Roy Stokes, School of Librarianship, Loughborough, England, for time and effort spent as liaison agent between committee and printers.

INTRODUCTION

"This play—as cast, acted, and produced, at the Theatre Royal, Drury Lane—
under the direction of Mr. Macready—was the most wonderfully perfect representation of court, and pastoral life, ever witnessed on the English Stage!"

GEORGE ELLIS

"Mr. Macready, falling in with this pictorial illustrating age, seems to pride
himself on leading the way in making all and every thing subservient to meretri-
cious ornament and show.—There never lived an actor or stage proprietor who
has done more injury to the drama in this respect than Mr. Macready."

WILLIAM ROBSON—*The Old Play-Goer*

The production of *As You Like It* which William Charles Macready staged in Drury Lane
Theatre during the season of 1842–43 was one of his most beautiful "illustrations" of
Shakespeare, and it was a significant event in the stage history of the play. Macready
"restored the true text" (as far as time and public morality permitted) in what then seemed
to be a revolutionary manner; and as a veteran producer of more than a dozen Shakespearean revivals at Covent Garden and Drury Lane he could apply to *As You Like It* his
fully matured directorial and managerial skills.

Unfortunately for Macready's reputation, the "pictorial illustrating age" (which The
Old Play-Goer complained of so bitterly) was only getting well under way, so that our
memory of Macready's scenic accomplishments in the 1830's and 1840's is obscured by
the far more lavish and more publicized stagings by Charles Kean in the 1850's. Macready
himself was scandalized at the lengths to which Kean would go, and told Lady Pollock that
he felt "in some measure responsible" for Kean's englutting of poetry and action in the
accessories: "I, in my endeavour to give to Shakespeare all his attributes, to enrich his
poetry with scenes worthy of its interpretation, to give to his tragedies their due magnificence, and to his comedies their entire brilliancy, have set an example which is accompanied
with great peril, for the public is willing to have the magnificence without the tragedy, and
the poet is swallowed up in display . . . . I am touched with a feeling something like remorse.

Is it possible, I ask myself. Did *I* hold the torch? Did *I* point out the path?" If Macready really did maintain a healthier balance between the "poetry" and "scenes worthy of its interpretation," as he here seems to claim, his work deserves better attention than it customarily has received from our theatre historians, whose accounts are often fragmentary, perfunctory, and sometimes vitiated by irresponsible guesswork.

The purpose of this volume, then, is twofold. It is, first, to provide in facsimile a significant specimen of a mid-nineteenth century prompt-book—Macready's *As You Like It* as transcribed by a responsible stage manager, George Ellis, for the instruction of an actor of the next generation, Hermann Vezin. Secondly, by means of the notes and illustrations inserted in the free spaces of the interleaves, I hope to have made it possible for the student of theatre history to reconstruct in his mind's eye the salient features of Macready's production. This is not a book to "read" but to "study." With the evidence here given (and a recording of the *Pastoral Symphony*), he who will can dream his very way nearly back to the Forest of Arden as it appeared on the stage of Drury Lane Theatre over a century ago.

The prompt-book record of this *As You Like It*, from Macready's first intentions to the production itself and beyond and after, is remarkably complete. These following are the more important documents which I have examined:

1. *Macready's preparation copy* (Library of the University of Illinois). This is a small interleaved volume of a popular reprint of the George Steevens edition, which contains Macready's prospective cuttings, scenic prescriptions, and stage business, written in ink in Macready's own hand. It is signed "W. C. Macready/Sept 8th 1842." It is the result of a month or more of summer planning which, as we read in Macready's *Diaries*, began on the evening of July 16 in the midst of a family vacation at Eastbourne.

2. *Willmott's prompt-book* (Folger Shakespeare Library). This is another interleaved Steevens text, somewhat larger than Macready's copy, labelled "Original prompt book." Here, in the clerkly hand of a professional copyist, is transcribed exactly all the matter in Macready's preparation copy. Further, it contains in a rough hand various notes, corrections, warning signals, timings, and the like. I call this "Willmott's prompt-book" because I am confident that it was the copy used by John Willmott, Macready's prompter, and that most of the additional jottings are by his hand.

3. *George Ellis's first prompt-book* (Folger Shakespeare Library). Willmott's prompt-book is apparently not final. Sometime during the season, or after, his assistant prompter, George Ellis, made up a "clean" copy, which I believe represents the play as it was actually played. It restores about eighty lines which Macready had originally inked out, and deletes about ninety-five which Macready had thought to retain (many of these ninety-five are in fact *pencilled* out in Macready's preparation copy.) It uses Macready's language to describe the scenery and the stage business, but with significant alterations, augmentations, and deletions, as if describing what *did* appear rather than what Macready had *foreseen* as appearing. It is magnificently professional in its record of entrances, crosses, exits, groove numbers, sound effects, character and property lists, warning signals, stage maps, and timings. Remarkably, however, this copy is executed in pencil, not ink, on interleaves of rather soft wove paper; and it does not show the soil of heavy thumbing as does Willmott's prompt-book. It would appear that Ellis made this copy for his own use, rather than for service in the prompter's box. Folded into it, though, are the

call sheets from which Ellis, or the call boy, sang out the actors' warnings at the green room doors. These too are in Ellis's hand—in ink on gray laid paper water-marked 1842; they are sewn together to make a tall, narrow twelve-page booklet. The booklet has been *very much used*: indeed, the inclusion of a scenic prescription on a scrap of note paper embossed "Windsor Castle" suggests that Ellis was working from the same call sheets on January 31, 1851, when he managed Charles Kean's performance of *As You Like It* for Queen Victoria at Windsor Castle. * * * Of the career of George Cressall Ellis (*c.* 1810–75) distressingly little is known, though his beautiful handwriting is "everywhere" in prompt-books of the period. According to his obituary notice in the *Times* on June 24, 1875, he died at West Brompton in his sixty-sixth year, and he was remembered as "for many years Director of Her Majesty's Dramatic Performances at Windsor Castle." From 1850 to 1859 he was Charles Kean's stage manager at the Princess's Theatre; he wrote two harlequinades which were produced there. Between 1848 and 1857 he served under Kean as Assistant Director (and keeper of the account books) of the Windsor Theatricals, a post in which he took great pride—"for it gave me a 'status' in the profession—at once enviable and distinguished—which I could not, perhaps, have otherwise attained." Later on he "directed" the Windsor Theatricals under the auspices of William Bodham Donne, who managed them after 1859. In his farewell note to Kean on August 29, 1859 (Folger Shakespeare Library), Ellis remarks that he entered the profession "now some Four and Thirty years ago." Whether his entering the profession was as a juvenile actor or as a callboy, the year would have been 1825, when he was about fifteen years of age. In the 1842–43 season, when he served under Macready at Drury Lane, he played small parts and served as Willmott's assistant. Evidently he remained at Drury Lane, as chief prompter, about four seasons longer, during which time he built up a library of perfected prompt-books, mainly derived from Macready's productions; and he would sometimes transcribe these for other actors, even occasionally providing water-colors of the scenery and costumes which Macready had used. He appears to have been a modest, self-effacing man, with a genius for exactitude and order, who raised the "custody of the book" to a highly responsible profession.

4. 5. *Charles Kean's prompt-books* (Folger Shakespeare Library). When Ellis became stage manager at the Princess's in 1850 one of his early duties was to prepare for Kean a faithful copy of Macready's book of *As You Like It* (transcribed from number 3, above). Remembering the cordial hostility that existed between Kean and Macready (they had had a vicious tiff over the arrangements of the Windsor Castle *Julius Caesar* less than a year before), one might wonder why Kean would want the copy. But this is to reckon without Kean's acquisitiveness. *As You Like It* is but the last in a long series (at least nine) of Macready's prompt-books which Ellis had been feeding to Kean since about 1845. Moreover, Kean was scheduled to take the play to Windsor during the 1850–51 series of Command performances, and he knew that he would have to present it in the form which the Queen and the Prince had seen and approved at Drury Lane eight years earlier. It was well that he was so foresighted. For the Queen seems to have sent warning to him, through her major-domo, Colonel Charles Phipps, that she would tolerate no indecencies. Among the Kean correspondence at the Folger Shakespeare Library there is a copy of Kean's response to the Colonel, dated January 13, 1851, assuring him that "Mrs Kean is very glad to be relieved of the Cuckoo song"—offering even to suppress the Epilogue, "as she fears that which is usually addressed to a public audience may appear offensive at Court." Ellis did not append Macready's name to Kean's copy, of course, but signed it "by George Ellis Theatres Royal Drury Lane & Covent Garden" and dated it 1850. Every detail of Macready's cutting and production plan is faithfully recorded, excepting, conspicuously, that after the first scene the groove numbers are omitted: the temporary stage in the Rubens Room at Windsor was not equipped with grooves, and all scenic effects were expressed on drop cloths rather than on sliding flats. * * * At the end of the decade Kean had another copy of *As You Like It* made up—"cut marked and corrected for Charles

Kean Esqr by T. W. Edmonds, Prompter Royal Princess's Theatre, London 1850 to 1859"—to record the play as he was accustomed to staging it. According to this copy, Kean rejected every one of Macready's corrections and restorations, and reverted wholesale to all the worst sins of the pre-Macready acting editions.

6. 7. 8. 9. *Samuel Phelps's and Henry Betty's prompt-books* (Folger Shakespeare Library.) Samuel Phelps, who played Adam in Macready's *As You Like It*, and who proceeded to a distinguished career as a producer of Shakespeare at Sadler's Wells Theatre, has left us two prompt-books: one, much used, is severally dated—on the cover and within—1848, 1852, 1857, 1858, and 1859; the other, a relatively clean copy, was probably made up later. Henry Betty, son of the famous "Young Roscius," William Henry West Betty, has left two nearly identical prompt-books, probably of the 1850's. Phelps did not ape Macready in *As You Like It*, but rather emulated him, working independently to create a similarly faithful text and original (more modest) techniques of staging it. Betty's books seem to follow Phelps's in many details, and to press on farther towards important restorations. But Betty remembered certain vivid details from Macready which Phelps omitted: he included Macready's beloved "sheep bells," and his construction of the Temple of Hymen in the final scene was markedly in the Macready manner. The significant thing about both Phelps and Betty is that, like Macready, they broke with the old acting editions and aimed to restore the Shakespearean text.

10. THE PROMPT-BOOK HERE REPRODUCED. *The Macready-Ellis-Vezin prompt-book* (Library of the University of Illinois). During the 1852-53 season, a young actor named Hermann Vezin was employed at the Princess's Theatre for a line of small supporting roles. Vezin was an American, born in Philadelphia in 1829, who after completing his M.A. degree at the University of Pennsylvania in 1850 had come to England to join the profession. He was to become in the later Victorian theatre something of what Macready had been in the earlier—"the most scholarly and intellectual actor of his generation," to quote the words of John Parker's *DNB* notice. It is therefore more delightful than surprising to discover that during his first decade in England young Vezin commissioned George Ellis to transcribe for him the prompt-books of the finest Shakespeare productions that Ellis had had access to. Nine of these, several of them derived from Macready originals, are in the Library of the University of Illinois, a gift of Ernest Ingold, founder of the Library's Ernest Ingold Shakespeare Collection. The Vezin book of *As You Like It* (watermarked 1848 and 1852 in the interleaves) is a faithful transcription of Ellis's own master copy (number 3, above). It is this book, with its elegantly drawn symbols and superb calligraphy, which I have elected to present in facsimile. It exactly represents Macready's production as Ellis first wrote it down; it testifies, through Vezin's later use of it, to the influence Macready exerted long after his retirement. It also memorializes an astonishing event—a scholarly and artist-like stage-manager is here seen in the very act of transmitting the thinking of a scholar-actor of one age to a scholar-actor of the next. Vezin played Orlando on various occasions while his youth was yet on him, as at Sadler's Wells with Samuel Phelps in 1860, and eventually he graduated to Jaques. His first metropolitan Jaques was, I believe, in February of 1875, and he subsequently repeated it in Marie Litton's revival in 1880 and in Hare and Kendal's revival in 1885. "His Jaques proved a singularly fine performance," says John Parker, "full of subtle irony, humour, and poetry." The reader will find here and there in the facsimile a roughly scribbled "in" and a few roughly scratched cuts: these markings are probably Vezin's. About thirty-five further markings by Vezin, faintly pencilled, have been suppressed from this reproduction. * * * The directions in Ellis's hand are consistent and clear throughout, though since he uses some stage abbreviations which are obsolete, a few "translations" are perhaps called for: *X^{es}* and *X^{ing}* of course mean "crosses" and "crossing"; *L2E* means "second entrance on stage left" (the space between the first and second sets of grooves), and *RUE* means "upper entrance on stage right"; *3.4.5. Gro^s* means "wings and flats set in the third,

fourth, and fifth grooves" (numbering from the front of the stage); a boxed *W* means "whistle"—i.e., the prompter's whistle to signal change of scene; *ACT* means "warn the curtain handler that the act is ending"; *AD* means "bring down the act drop." For some reason Ellis dispenses with the prompter's bell: such common symbols of the day as *Ring*, *RAB* ("ring act bell"), and *RMB* ("ring music bell") do not appear in this book at all. An oddity of Ellis's handwriting is that the capital letters *C* and *E* and his small *b* look very much alike. The *E* (often used for "Entrance") may be distinguished by the tiny dot within its upper loop.

11. 12. 13. *Further prompt-books derived from the originals.* Other actors or managers from time to time transcribed Macready's arrangements. Those who knew no better would take the traditionally corrupted pre-Macready acting version ("as performed at the Theatres 'Royal"), patch onto it Macready's directions, and more or less restore the missing "Shakespeare" in long hand. Unfortunately for the profession, Macready's acting version never passed into print. In 1857 or later Thomas Hailes Lacy, in his *Acting Edition of Plays*, published a text prefaced by a transcript of Macready's playbill, and this has been commonly taken for Macready's version (*e.g.*, by Professor Odell, *Shakespeare from Betterton to Irving*, II, 205). But Lacy's text was only a catchpenny reprinting of the traditional stage version, not reflecting Macready's restoration at all, and of no help to the profession. One of these "restored-corrupted" copies, now in the New York Public Library, was "marked from Drury Lane Prompt Bk, London 1842": this was made on the "bad" text of *French's Standard Drama* by John Moore, an Anglo-American prompter and indefatigable traditionalist, who about 1848 brought a great collection of transcriptions of London stagings to America, and who forty years later was responsible for the text and business of the Augustin Daly-Ada Rehan *As You Like It*. (The date 1842 is, of course, the date of the original, not the date of transcription. And this copy, although it is in Moore's hand, is obviously not Moore's *first* copy, for the imprint of *French's Standard Drama* did not appear until long after Moore came to America. Incidentally, this is one of the *As You Like It* prompt-books described by Professor W. G. B. Carson in the *Quarterly Journal of Speech*, April, 1957, and there tentatively ascribed to Alfred Bunn.) Another of John Moore's copies, based on the "bad" text of the *Modern Standard Drama*, 1848, is in the Folger Shakespeare Library. Another copy, made from one or another of these Moore books by James Taylor, is owned by Professor Alan Downer of Princeton University. Other similar "Macready" prompt-books of *As You Like It* are doubtless extant – none of them of great worth intrinsically, but each interesting as an echo, however distant, of Macready's way of doing it in 1842.

In preparing his stage version of *As You Like It*, Macready's aims were to reduce the bulk of the text to practical dimensions for performance in Drury Lane Theatre, to expurgate such parts as would offend his extremely decorous audience, and to "restore" the play—*i.e.*, to restore the order of the scenes and to get rid of flagrant corruptions which the theatrical profession had foisted upon the play during the preceding century. Three then well-known editions of the traditionally corrupted "acting copy" of the play are those of Mrs. Inchbald in *The British Theatre* (1808), William Oxberry in *English Drama* (1819), and John Cumberland (1826), all of which stem from, and "improve upon," John Bell's edition, "as performed at the Theatre-Royal, Drury Lane," in 1773. Avoiding these (which he knew by heart), Macready took a "true text" of the play and started fresh. In cutting for time, he did not have to butcher the play as certain later producers in the days of heavy three-dimensional scenery were wont to do, for the wing and groove system of scenic decoration, which still prevailed, afforded instantaneous changes in full view of the audience, and allowed almost perfectly continuous playing. Shakespeare's text is reckoned at 2,845 lines (this is Professor G. B. Harrison's count): Macready cut only 387, reducing the total to 2,458 lines. As has been noted above, Macready did not strictly abide by his fresh cutting: when we compare his preparation copy with Ellis's final prompt-book we observe a tendency to revert to some of the major time-saving excisions dictated by tradition. His expurgations for propriety's sake and his major restorations I have called attention to in the notes interspersed throughout the text. The playing time, as Ellis records it, was two hours and forty-nine minutes, or "3 Hours.—Includg waits." The "waits" in those days were not protracted "intervals" as in the modern theatre, but tiny entr'actes of two to five minutes to mark the act-ends and sometimes to cover scenery and costume change. On June 12, 1843, after the twenty-second and final performance of *As You Like It*, Prince Albert asked Macready if this was not the "original play." Macready could fairly answer, yielding what must be yielded to the times and manners, "Yes, that we had restored the original text."

The reader who seeks enlightenment in the mysteries of wing and groove scenery must turn to Richard Southern's exhaustive work on that subject, called *Changeable Scenery*. It must suffice here to say that for the most part scenery consisted of perspective painting on flat canvas surfaces which stood or hung parallel to the curtain-line. Occasionally, as in the second and last scenes of Macready's *As You Like It*, the main picture was painted on a large cloth called a "drop," which in these instances was hung at the back of the stage. More often the picture was painted on a "pair of flats" (at Drury Lane Theatre these were two canvas-covered frames, each 21 feet tall and 14 feet wide) which slid on stage in floor grooves and met at center; if the flats were in upstage grooves they would be complemented by "wings", 21 feet tall and some 5 to 8 feet wide, in downstage grooves, and by corresponding "borders" hung above. An effect of depth and distance could be obtained by the use of "cut flats" standing in front of solid flats—the cut flats presenting, for instance, seemingly free-standing trees and bushes. "Set pieces" (three-dimensional units) could be used occasionally, and in this production were apparently used rather sparingly. For quick reference I include here plates of the ground plan and longitudinal section of Drury Lane Theatre as published by Charles Dibdin in his *History and Illustrations of the London Theatres* (1826). Whether these are exactly representative of the stage as Macready used it in 1842 is questionable, but at least one can be confident of certain major features: the forestage was over 12 feet deep; the proscenium opening was 40 feet wide at the curtain-line, but reduceable to about 35 feet by movable panels; the stage behind the curtain-line, conspicuously raked, was some 48 feet deep and over 80 feet from wall to wall; there were scene docks at either side. Dibdin's representation of the grooves is dubious, for such stage machinery was always being revised. Six sets of grooves are pictured here. In *As You Like It* Ellis never refers to grooves farther upstage than the fifth; yet in *King John*, which Macready produced three weeks later, there were scenes "set to the seventh groove." We gather from the second scene of *As You Like It* that all the floor-surface upstage of the third grooves was trapped or removable. It is important to remember (as Dibdin's plates do not show at all) that the floor grooves were matched by overhead grooves fixed under the floor of the fly-galleries at either side of the stage, which held the wings and flats vertical and guided them in their sliding; and furthermore that the overhead grooves were equipped with hinged extensions which when dropped into place would guide the pairs of flats all the way to the center of the stage. A complete flat scene could be thrust on in any pair of grooves. The scenic artists preferred the upstage grooves, but occasional brief scenes occurred even in the first grooves, the generous forestage allowing the actors plenty of room to keep out of each other's way. The use of "front scenes" or "carpenters' scenes," as first-groove scenes were often called, made possible the discovery of elaborately furnished or numerously peopled scenes in the upstage areas.

The scenery which Macready prescribed was designed and painted by Charles Marshall (1806–90), the principal scenic artist of Drury Lane Theatre and one of the best of the day. Trained under John Wilson at Astley's Amphitheatre and Marinari at Drury Lane, he had served at various minor houses before coming into his own under Macready's management of Covent Garden (1837–39) and Drury Lane (1841–43). During these years he decorated most of Macready's major productions, both revivals and new plays. After Macready withdrew from management, Marshall became the scenic artist for the opera at Her Majesty's Theatre in the Haymarket, where he served from 1844 to 1858. He was also a distinguished landscape painter. Marshall's credit for *As You Like It* has often been denied him by careless writers who ascribe it to the more famous artist Clarkson Stanfield. Macready had indeed at times turned to Stanfield, an old and dear friend, to bolster the reputation of his scenic department by "illustrating" a production (a Christmas pantomime in 1837, the dioramas for the choruses of *Henry V* in June, 1839; the opera of *Acis and Galatea* in February, 1842). On July 10 and 29, 1842, as we read in the *Diaries*, he had consulted Stanfield about *As You Like It*, and in the fall of 1842 Stanfield was often backstage, along with other of Macready's friends, as an unofficial adviser. But Charles Marshall was the artist. Examination of the playbills reveals that, although the first two do not mention scenery at all, beginning with the bill of October 6 every one of them bears the line, just above the *dramatis personae*, "The SCENERY by Mr. MARSHALL." Marshall painted ten complete settings: Oliver's house in the orchard, the palace exterior, a room inside the palace, and seven scenes in the Forest of Arden (including one of Rosalind's cottage, one showing a sheepfold in the distance, and one called "The Beechen Avenue"). Marshall must also have designed the demountable set piece described as "a kind of rural temple" which the dancing shepherds erected for the Masque of Hymen near the end of the play. His scenery was immensely impressive to its beholders. "So far as stage pictures may be made to contribute to dramatic illusion," said the *Athenaeum* reviewer, "the scenery, and its adjuncts, supply to the outward senses some such images as appear to the mind's eye of the reader," and "we are ready to exclaim with Touchstone, 'Now I am in Arden.' " The *Spectator's* account is especially vivid: "*As You Like It* was represented on this occasion as the poet wrote it, for the first time in the memory of the present generation of playgoers, and, it may be said without presumption, as he would have wished to see it represented— at least so far as the scenic accessories are concerned. The spectacle is not merely correct and elegant, but suggestive; aiding the fancy in realizing the local and other characteristics of every scene, according to the poetic indications of the dialogue. The architectural views are designed in the old French style; and the sylvan scenes have a wild and primitive aspect, denoting the remoteness and seclusion of that 'desert inaccessible' the Forest of Arden: old trees of giant growth spread their gnarled and knotted arms, forming a 'shade of melancholy boughs' for the banished Duke and his sylvan court; the swift brook brawls along its pebbly bed; the sheep-bell's 'drowsy tinkling' is heard from the fold on the hill-side; and the lodge in the wilderness, overgrown with creeping plants, is musical with birds . . . The last scene, a stately vista of lofty trees, in which a floral temple is erected by the foresters for Hymen's altar, is a pretty fancy in pastoral taste. In short nothing is wanting to complete the scenic pictures; nor is anything overdone." One of the scenes— that of the wrestling match on the terrace in front of the ducal palace—has been preserved for us in T. H. Shepherd's pretty drawing of the interior of Drury Lane Theatre during performance.

The costume designs here presented (now in the Library of the University of Illinois) were recently discovered by Macready's granddaughter, Mrs. Lisa Puckle. Apparently these eight are all that have survived. They are the work of Colonel Charles Hamilton Smith (1776–1859) of Plymouth, a scientist and antiquarian who retired from the army in 1820 to devote himself to writing on such diverse subjects as military history, the natural history of dogs, horses, and man, and the history of costume. Macready had often turned to him for period costume designs and other historical data; in the 1850's Charles Kean relied upon Smith and his daughter Emma for information about innumerable details of ancient dress, armor, heraldic blazonry, and the like in his elaborate productions at the Princess's Theatre. The principles for costuming *As You Like It* "historically" had been laid down in 1824 by James Robinson Planché in booklet Number 3 of a series called *Dramatic Costume*. Planché was the first to dress the play according to authentic originals of late fifteenth century France (specifically, the reign of Charles VIII), and in this dating

Smith apparently followed Planché's lead. Planché's court costume designs are very beautiful—exquisite in draughtsmanship and brilliantly tinted (the colors are laid on by hand). One senses though that he was not much interested in the sartorial aspects of the play once it settled into the Forest of Arden. Among his eighteen plates there is but one "hunting costume" (green tights, green jacket with yellow collar, black hat with green feathers) to be worn indiscriminately by all the exiled courtiers—including Jaques! Smith, of course, provided a very special and handsome costume for Macready's Jaques; an interesting, if somewhat fussy, costume for Rosalind-Ganymede (Planché neglected Ganymede altogether); and a Touchstone garb far more distinctive than Planché's conventional "motley."

As for Macready's over-all art as director-producer, the critic of *John Bull* waxed the most eloquent, praising his "delicacy of appreciation, soundness of judgment, and grasp of execution." Whatever were the flaws of detail—and *John Bull* found many—yet "divested of the antiquated sentimentality of the old stage directions, almost every scene is a new creation. It is a most masterly piece of histrionic art. It will aid the imagination when reading the poet hereafter, and assist the fancy to supply those accessories which, from the nature of all dramatic writing, are necessary to be pictured before its beauties can be fully appreciated."

I am grateful to Mrs. Lisa Puckle, of Pirbright, Surrey, for making available to me the costume designs of her grandfather's *As You Like It*; to Mrs. Mary Reardon Keating of the Harvard Theatre Collection, to Mr. George Nash of the Gabrielle Enthoven Collection, to Miss Isabelle Grant of the Library of the University of Illinois, and to Miss Dorothy Mason and the staff of the Folger Shakespeare Library for their painstaking and generous assistance in research; to Professor Alan S. Downer of Princeton University for invaluable encouragement and guidance towards important sources; to my colleagues, Professors Gwynne Evans, Barnard Hewitt, and Wesley Swanson for criticism of the work while it was in progress; to the Graduate College Research Board of the University of Illinois for a study grant; to the Directors of the Folger Shakespeare Library for a Fellowship under which I have been able to read in the magnificent prompt-book collection of that library; and to the officers of Beta Phi Mu for undertaking the publishment of this book.

CHARLES H. SHATTUCK
The University of Illinois
March 3, 1961

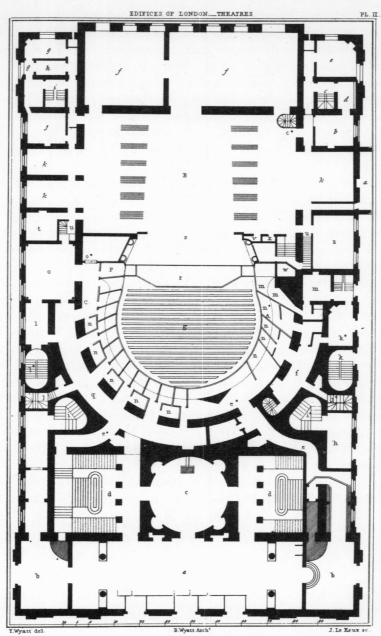

T. Wyatt del.   B. Wyatt Arch[t]   J. Le Keux sc.

DRURY LANE THEATRE,
PLAN.

PROOF   M[c] QUEEN

London, Published Jan.1825, by J. Taylor, High Holborn.

T. Wyatt del.ᵗ

B. Wyatt Arch.ᵗ

J. Le Keux sc.

McQUEEN.

DRURY LANE THEATRE,

LONGITUDINAL SECTION FROM EAST TO WEST.

London, Published Jan. 1825, by J Taylor, High Holborn.

PROOF

AS YOU LIKE IT.

VOL. XIII.   A

PERSONS OF THE DRAMA.

Theatre Royal,
Drury Lane. *1841=2.*

DUKE, *living in Exile.*   Mr Ryder.

FREDERICK, *Brother to the* DUKE, *and Usurper of his Dominions.*   " G Bennett.

AMIENS, } *Lords attending upon the Duke in his Ba-*
JAQUES, }   *nishment.*   " Allen
     " Macready.

LE BEAU, *a Courtier attending upon* FREDERICK.   " Hudson

CHARLES, *his Wrestler.*   " Howell.

OLIVER,
JAQUES, } *Sons of Sir* ROWLAND DE BOIS.   " Graham. R.
ORLANDO,   " Lynne.
     " Anderson.

ADAM, } *Servants to* OLIVER.   " Phelps.
DENNIS,   " J Ellis.

TOUCHSTONE, *a Clown.*   " Keeley

Sir OLIVER MAR-TEXT, *a Vicar.*   " H Mellon.

CORIN, } *Shepherds.*   " H Bennett.
SILVIUS,   " Stanton

WILLIAM, *A Country Fellow, in love with* AUDREY.   " Compton

A Person representing HYMEN.   Miss P Horton.

ROSALIND, *Daughter to the banished* DUKE.   Mrs Nisbett

CELIA, *Daughter to* FREDERICK.   " Stirling.

PHEBE, *a Shepherdess.*

AUDREY, *a Country Wench.*   " Keeley.

Lords belonging to the two Dukes ; Pages, Foresters, and other Attendants.   [H Phillips, Lenn Reeves, Stretton S Jones, Redfern, Clifford,

The SCENE *lies, first, near* OLIVER'S *House; afterwards partly in the Usurper's Court, and partly in the Forest of Arden.*

AS YOU LIKE IT

THE DRAMATIS PERSONAE

(from the playbill of October 1, 1842)

Duke, *living in exile*   Mr. RYDER

(*His first appearance.*)

First Lord		Mr. ELTON
Second Lord	*Lords attending upon the Duke in his banishment*	Mr. H. PHILLIPS
Amiens		Mr. ALLEN
Jaques		Mr. MACREADY

Duke Frederick, *Brother to the rightful Duke, & usurper of his dominions*   Mr. G. BENNETT

Le Beau, *a Courtier attending upon Frederick*   Mr. HUDSON

Charles, *his wrestler*   Mr. HOWELL

Oliver		Mr. GRAHAM
Jaques	*Sons of Sir Rowland de Bois*	Mr. LYNNE
Orlando		Mr. ANDERSON

Adam	*Servants to Oliver*	Mr. PHELPS
Dennis		Mr. ELLIS

Touchstone, *a Clown*   Mr. KEELEY

Sir Oliver Mar-Text, *a Vicar*   Mr. MELLON

Corin	*Shepherds*	Mr. W. BENNETT
Sylvius		Mr. STANTON

William, *a country fellow, in love with Audrey*   Mr. COMPTON

Pages, *attending upon the banished Duke*   Miss P. HORTON
                                               Miss GOULD

Lords, *attending Duke Frederick*

> Mr. ROBERTS, Mr. WALDRON, Mr. BENDER, Mr. C. J. SMITH, Mr. CARLE, Mr. HARCOURT, Mr. SEVIER, Mr. STILT, &c.

Lords, *attending the banished Duke*

> Mr. REDFEARN, Mr. YARNOLD, Mr. S. JONES, Messrs. Walsh, May, J. Beale, Walker, Collett, Leigh, Gilbeigh, Simmons, George, Price, T. Price, Macarthy, Barclay, Cowbrick, Miller, &c.

Foresters

> Mr. STRETTON, Mr. J. REEVES, Messrs. Clifford, Hance, Hill, Pigeon, Wemis, Johnson, Tyrrell, Foster, Richards, Ryan, &c.

Shepherds

> Messrs. Paulo, Brady, Roffey, Burdett, Sharpe, Priorson, Gouriet, King, Gilbert, J. Roffey, Lake, Upsdell, &c.

Rosalind, *Daughter to the banished Duke*   Mrs. NISBETT
> *(Her first appearance here these Six Years.)*

Celia, *Daughter to Duke Frederick*   Mrs. STIRLING
Phebe, *a Shepherdess*   Miss E. PHILLIPS

> *(In consequence of the illness of Miss Fortescue.)*

Audrey, *a Country Wench*   Mrs. KEELEY

Ladies of the Court

> Mesdames Byers, C. Byers, Goward, Perry, Boden, Smith, Foster, Newcombe, King, Mapleson, Williams, Jackson, &c.

Shepherdesses

> Miss WEBSTER, Mesdames Maile, Reede, Greene, Sutton, Berringer, Carson, Lee, Hunt, Schmidt, T. Marsano, Travis, A. Travis, &c. &c.

———

As You Like It was performed twenty-two times during the season: October 1, 4, 6, 8, 12, 14, 19, 21, 26, November 2, 9, 17, 24, December 1, 7, 29, January 4, February 1, 22, March 25, May 27 ("positively last time"), and June 12 (Royal Command). From time to time there were alterations in the cast. After the second performance Miss E. Phillips yielded Phebe to Mrs. Serle, who played it from October 6 to December 7; Miss Fortescue, who was originally intended for Phebe, took up the part on December 29 and played the remaining seven performances. Helen Faucit displaced Mrs. Nisbett as Rosalind on December 1 and 7 and June 12. Miss Ellis displaced Mrs. Stirling as Celia on June 12. The name of H. Phillips (Second Lord) disappears from December 29 on, as do also the names of sixty-odd minor performers (Forest Lords, Shepherds, Ladies of the Court, etc.) in order to make room for the elaborate description of the Christmas pantomime. On a couple of occasions Lynne replaced Graham as Oliver, and W. H. Bland was assigned to Jaques de Bois; Bland played Charles the wrestler in the final performance. On February 1 Macready, being then in the throes of preparing Browning's *A Blot on the 'Scutcheon*, yielded Jaques (for this one performance only) to Mr. Elton.

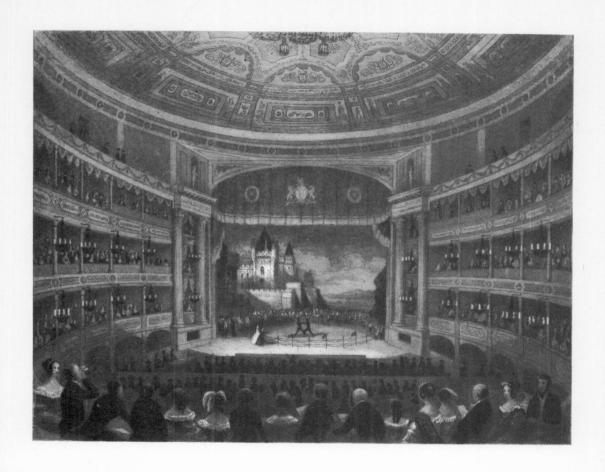

THE WRESTLING SCENE

T. H. Shepherd's drawing of the interior of Drury Lane Theatre
during a performance of *As You Like It*.

THE STAGING OF I. 1 (179 lines). The act drop rose to discover Orlando and Adam in the orchard of Oliver's house. Flats in the second grooves and wings in the first grooves represented the orchard, some part of the house at stage left, and probably ornamental gateposts at stage right. The house (in the second entrance left) was probably a three-dimensional set piece mounted on rollers. Traditionally this scene had been split in two, the action moving inside the house at line 92 ("Hola, Dennis!", page 8) in order to justify the words "here at the door" at line 96. The eighteenth century adaptors would not have known that in Elizabethan stage parlance "door" meant simply "stage-door." Macready preserved verisimilitude by altering the phrase to "here at the gate." Macready originally cut some twenty-one lines from this scene, but apparently restored them all.

Ⓧ / The House - as within the Orchard - is L-2 E,- The entrance - as from the road to the grounds, - is R.- /

I.-

Orlando.
Adam.
Oliver.

ACT. I. SCENE. II.

HOWARD, A.R.A. PINXIT.   PUBLISHED BY LONGMAN & CO. MDCCCVII.   BROMLEY, SCULPSIT.

AS YOU LIKE IT.

ACT I.

SCENE I.—*An Orchard, near* OLIVER'S *House.*

~~Enter~~ ORLANDO *and* ADAM.

Orl. As I remember, Adam, it was upon this fashion
bequeathed me: By will, but a poor thousand crowns;
and, as thou say'st, charged my brother, on his bless-
ing, to breed me well: and there begins my sadness.

My brother Jaques he keeps at school, and report speaks
goldenly of his profit: for my part, he keeps me rusti-
cally at home, or, to speak more properly, stays me
here at home unkept: For call you that keeping for a
gentleman of my birth, that differs not from the stall-
ing of an ox? His horses are bred better; for, besides
that they are fair with their feeding, they are taught
their manage, and to that end riders dearly hired: but
I, his brother, gain nothing under him but growth; for
the which his animals on his dunghills are as much
bound to him as I. Besides this nothing, that he so
plentifully gives me, the something, that nature gave
me, his countenance seems to take from me: he lets
me feed with his hinds, bars me the place of a brother,
and, as much as in him lies, mines my gentility with
my education. This is it, Adam, that grieves me; and
the spirit of my father, which I think is within me, begins to mutiny against this servitude: I will no longer
endure it, though yet I know no wise remedy how to
avoid it.

Enter OLIVER.

Adam. Yonder comes my master, your brother.
Orl. Go apart, Adam, and thou shalt hear how he
will shake me up.
Oli. Now, sir! what make you here?
Orl. Nothing: I am not taught to make any thing.
Oli. What mar you then, sir?
Orl. Marry, sir, I am helping you to mar that which
God made, a poor unworthy brother of yours, with
idleness.

2.

[Dennis. /2ᵃ/

Charles. /Act./]

Q /Adam retires a little, up C,— somewhat reluctantly, and with an anxiety of manner./

GOD AND HEAVEN. The name of God was not spoken from the stage (in dramatic dialogue, that is) in Macready's day, the word "Heaven" usually being substituted for it. In this prompt-book "God" is suppressed seventeen times.

ORLANDO'S ATTACK. In speculating on how this physical encounter was traditionally managed, Professor A. C. Sprague says, "Oliver, one is sure, is the first to pass from words to deeds" (*Shakespeare and the Actors*, p. 31). But here Orlando is obviously the aggressor. Oliver is crossing impatiently to stage left, and on the word "young", Orlando "lays hold" of him—with a firm locking grip, too, which precludes much resistance from Oliver, for Orlando commands the dialogue down to "releases him."

Q /Lays hold of Oliver, as he passes him./

∧ /advances C.-/

∧ /releases him./

Oli. Marry, sir, be better employ'd, and be naught awhile.

Orl. Shall I keep your hogs, and eat husks with them? What prodigal portion have I spent, that I should come to such penury?

Oli. Know you where you are, sir?

Orl. O, sir, very well: here in your orchard.

Oli. Know you before whom, sir?

Orl. Ay, better than he I am before knows me. I know, you are my eldest brother; and in the gentle condition of blood, you should so know me: The courtesy of nations allows you my better, in that you are the first-born; but the same tradition takes not away my blood, were there twenty brothers betwixt us: I have as much of my father in me as you: albeit, I confess, your coming before me is nearer to his reverence.

Oli. What, boy! /ẍ'u ℓ.⁻/

Orl. Come, come, elder brother, you are too young ⊗ in this.

Oli. Wilt thou lay hands on me, villain?

Orl. I am no villain: I am the yonngest son of sir Rowland de Bois; he was my father; and he is thrice a villain, that says, such a father begot villains: Wert thou not my brother, I would not take this hand from thy throat, till this other had pulled out thy tongue for saying so: thou hast railed on thyself.

Adam. Sweet masters, be patient; for your father's remembrance, be at accord.

Oli. Let me go, I say.

Orl. I will not, till I please: you shall hear me. My father charged you in his will to give me good education: you have trained me like a peasant, obscuring

and hiding from me all gentleman-like qualities: the
spirit of my father grows strong in me, and I will no
longer endure it: therefore allow me such exercises as
may become a gentleman, or give me the poor allottery
my father left me by testament; with that I will go
buy my fortunes.

Oli. And what wilt thou do? beg, when that is spent?
Well, sir, get you in: I will not long be troubled with
you: you shall have some part of your will: I pray you,
leave me.

Orl. I will no further offend you than becomes me
for my good.

Oli. Get you with him, you old dog.

Adam. Is old dog my reward? Most true, I have lost
my teeth in your service.——God be with my old master! he would not have spoke such a word.

[*Exeunt* Orlando and ADAM.

Oli. Is it even so? begin you to grow upon me? I
will physick your rankness, and yet give no thousand
crowns neither.   Hola, Dennis!

Enter DENNIS.

Den. Calls your worship?

Oli. Was not Charles, the Duke's wrestler, here to
speak with me?

Den. So please you, he is here at the door, and im-
portunes access to you.

Oli. Call him in.   [*Exit* DENNIS.]——'Twill be a good
way; and to-morrow the wrestling is.

∧ /X'es beh^d Grl' to R.- /

⊘ / Exit L-2 E.- /

⊙ / As Glwer X'es to L. corner,- Dennis enters hastily, R,- and is passing a X to the house,- not seeing Glwer./

Ø /Dennis precedes him, and then Exit's R:/

# #

March, and Shouts.
ready under the Stage.
/4 times:/

B.

Rosalind
Celia. gold chain.
Le Beau. /Shalln./
Duke Fred.ᵏ /Shalln./   } /2ᵈ:/
Touchstone.
Jester's Staff./
Orlando -
1ˢᵗ Court Lord. /Att./
2ⁿᵈ Do Do
/Shalln./
20 Court Lords. /2ᵃ/
20 Do Ladies.
/2 or 3 have Shalln./
12 Attendants
/Poles, &c for "Fling."/
6 pages

Enter CHARLES. *R.-* Q

Cha. Good morrow to your worship.

Oli. Good monsieur Charles!—what's the new news at the new court?

Cha. There's no news at the court, sir, but the old news: that is, the old duke is banish'd by his younger brother the new duke; and three or four loving lords have put themselves into voluntary exile with him, whose lands and revenues enrich the new duke; therefore he gives them good leave to wander.

Oli. Can you tell, if Rosalind, the duke's daughter, be banished with her father?

Cha. O, no; for the duke's daughter, her cousin, so loves her,—being ever from their cradles bred together,—that she would have followed her exile, or have died to stay behind her. She is at the court, and no less beloved of her uncle than his own daughter; and never two ladies loved as they do.

Oli. Where will the old duke live?

Cha. They say, he is already in the forest of Arden, and a many merry men with him: and there they live like the old Robin Hood of England: they say, many young gentlemen flock to him every day; and fleet the time carelessly, as they did in the golden world.

Oli. What, you wrestle to-morrow before the new duke?

Cha. Marry, do I, sir; and I came to acquaint you with a matter. I am given, sir, secretly to understand, that your younger brother, Orlando, hath a disposition to come in disguis'd against me, to try a fall: To-morrow, sir, I wrestle for my credit; and he, that escapes

me without some broken limb, shall acquit him well.
Your brother is but young, and tender; and, for your
love, I would be loath to foil him, as I must, for my
own honour, if he come in: therefore, out of my love
to you, I came hither to acquaint you withal; that
either you might stay him from his intendment, or
brook such disgrace well as he shall run into; in that
it is a thing of his own search, and altogether against
my will.

Oli. Charles, I thank thee for thy love to me, which
thou shalt find I will most kindly requite. I had myself notice of my brother's purpose herein, and have by
underhand means laboured to dissuade him from it;
but he is resolute. I'll tell thee, Charles,—it is the
stubbornest young fellow of France; full of ambition,
an envious emulator of every man's good parts, a se-
cret and villainous contriver against me his natural brother; therefore use thy discretion; I had as lief thou
didst break his neck as his finger: And thou wert best
look to't; for if thou dost him any slight disgrace, or
if he do not mightily grace himself on thee, he will
practise against thee by poison, entrap thee by some
treacherous device, and never leave thee till he hath
ta'en thy life by some indirect means or other: for, I
assure thee, and almost with tears I speak it, there is
not one so young and so villainous this day living. I
speak but brotherly of him; but should I anatomize
him to thee as he is, I must blush and weep, and thou
must look pale and wonder.

Cha. I am heartily glad I came hither to you: If he
come to-morrow, I'll give him his payment: If ever he

⊘ _Set of the entire Stage. - The palace is on R.- A Turret Entrance, is steps._
R - 3 Ent^{ce}. - The Stage open at back, C.- and steps, R & L, as leading to a
Terrace, and the Grounds, below.

♯♯ _As the Scene opens, - March and Shouts heard,-_
very faintly, - as at a distance.

THE STAGING OF I. 2 (301 lines cut to 274). The orchard flats drew off at the prompter's whistle to reveal this "Set of the entire Stage," while march music and shouts were heard from far off. At the back of the stage, about forty-eight feet from the curtain line, hung a vast drop scene (see Shepherd's drawing), showing on its stage right half a portion of the palace and on the left a vista of low hills and clouded sky; the palace was brought forward on stage right by wing pieces, including in the third groove a turret entrance (with practical steps going up to it); "wood wings" were in the left grooves. The forestage and downstage area was called the "Terrace"; beyond the third grooves open traps uncovered "Terrace steps" leading down to the supposed sunken palace grounds.

go alone again, I'll never wrestle for prize more: And so, ~~God~~ *Heaven* ∧ keep your worship !   [*Exit. R.*]

Oli. Farewell, good Charles.—Now will I stir this gamester: I hope, I shall see an end of him; for my soul, yet I know not why, hates nothing more than he. Yet he's gentle; never school'd, and yet learned; full of noble device; of all sorts enchantingly beloved; and, indeed, so much in the heart of the world, and especially of my own people, who best know him, that I am altogether misprised: but it shall not be so long; this wrestler shall clear all: nothing remains, but that I kindle the boy thither, which now I'll go about.

[*Exit. L-2 E.*]

SCENE II.—*A Lawn before the Duke's Palace.*

Enter ROSALIND *and* CELIA. *Turret steps, R-3 E.*

Cel. I pray thee, Rosalind, sweet my coz, be merry.

Ros. Dear Celia, I show more mirth than I am mistress of; and would you yet I were merrier? Unless you could teach me to forget a banish'd father, you must not learn me how to remember any extraordinary pleasure.

Cel. Herein, I see, thou lovest me not with the full weight that I love thee: if my uncle, thy banished father, had banished thy uncle, the duke my father, so thou had been still with me, I could have taught my love to take thy father for mine; so would'st thou, if the truth of thy love to me were so righteously temper'd as mine is to thee.

12.-

Ros. Well, I will forget the condition of my estate, to rejoice in yours.

1.-

Cel. You know, my father hath no child but I, nor none is like to have; and, truly, when he dies, thou shalt be his heir: for what he hath taken away from thy father perforce, I will render thee again in affection; by mine honour, I will: and when I break that oath, let me turn monster: therefore, my sweet Rose, my dear Rose, be merry.

Ros. From henceforth I will, coz, and devise sports: let me see; What think you of falling in love?

Cel. Marry, I pr'ythee, do, to make sport withal: but love no man in good earnest; nor no further in sport neither, than with safety of a pure blush thou may'st in honour come off again.

Ros. What shall be our sport then?

Cel. Let us sit and mock the good housewife, Fortune, from her wheel, that her gifts may henceforth be bestowed equally.

Ros. I would, we could do so; for her benefits are mightily misplaced: and the bountiful blind woman doth most mistake in her gifts to women.

Cel. 'Tis true: for those, that she makes fair, she scarce makes honest; and those, that she makes honest, she makes very ill-favour'dly.

Ros. Nay, now thou goest from fortune's office to nature's: fortune reigns in gifts of the world, not in the lineaments of nature.

Enter TOUCHSTONE. /up terrace steps, L C./

Cel. No? When nature hath made a fair creature, may she not by fortune fall into the fire?—Though na-

⫫⫫

——————————→ —— *March and Shouts, -*

a little nearer, - and cont^d till Touchstone

in front.

Ɒ | Touch' appears - on ent'g - to be looking for some one. |

☉ | Cel' X'es C, - and Touch' ad's 'L - when she addresses him. |

∧ | Ros' and Cel' both laugh. |

| March g-Trotts, - nearer, -
and continued until Le
Beau is in front.

ture hath given us wit to flout at fortune, hath not fortune sent in this fool to cut off the argument?

Ros. Indeed, there is fortune too hard for nature;
when fortune makes nature's natural the cutter off of
nature's wit.

Cel. Peradventure, this is not fortune's work neither,
but nature's; who, perceiving our natural wits too dull
to reason of such goddesses, hath sent this natural for
our whetstone: for always the dulness of the fool is the
whetstone of his wits.—How now, wit? whither wander you?

Touch. Mistress, you must come away to your father.

Cel. Were you made the messenger?

Touch. No, by mine honour; but I was bid to come
for you.

Ros. Where learned you that oath, fool?

Touch. Of a certain knight, that swore by his honour
they were good pancakes, and swore by his honour the
mustard was naught: now, I'll stand to it, the pancakes
were naught, and the mustard was good; and yet was
not the knight forsworn.

Cel. How prove you that, in the great heap of your
knowledge?

Ros. Ay, marry; now unmuzzle your wisdom.

Touch. Stand you both forth now: stroke your chins,
and swear by your beards that I am a knave.

Cel. By our beards, if we had them, thou art.

Touch. By my knavery, if I had it, then I were: but
if you swear by that that is not, you are not forsworn:
no more was this knight, swearing by his honour, for
he never had any; or if he had, he had sworn it away,
before ever he saw those pancakes or that mustard.

Cel. Pr'ythee, who is't that thou mean'st?

Touch. One that old Frederick, your father, loves.

Cel. My father's love is enough to honour him. Enough! speak no more of him; you'll be whipp'd for taxation, one of these days.

Touch. The more pity, that fools may not speak wisely, what wise men do foolishly.

Cel. By my troth, thou say'st true: for since the little wit, that fools have, was silenced, the little foolery, that wise men have, makes a great show. Here comes Monsieur Le Beau.

Celia.

Enter LE BEAU, *up terrace steps, L.-*

Ros. With his mouth full of news.

Cel. Which he will put on us, as pigeons feed their young.

Ros. Then shall we be news-cramm'd.

Cel. All the better; we shall be the more marketable. *Bon jour*, Monsieur Le Beau: What's the news?

Le Beau. Fair princess, you have lost much good sport.

Cel. Sport? Of what colour?

Le Beau. What colour, madam? How shall I answer you?

Ros. As wit and fortune will.

Touch. Or as the destinies decree.

Cel. Well said; that was laid on with a trowel.

Touch. Nay, if I keep not my rank,——

Ros. Thou losest thy old smell.

Le Beau. You amaze me, ladies: I would have told you of good wrestling, which you have lost the sight of.

Ros. Yet tell us the manner of the wrestling.

Ros   bel   Le B.   Touch.
 o   o   o   o

R.-_____ L.-

March f-Fronts,
forte, - and cont d
till all on.

Le Beau. I will tell you the beginning, and, if it please your ladyships, you may see the end; for the best is yet to ·do; and here, where you are, they are coming to perform it.

Cel. Well,—the beginning, that is dead and buried.

Le Beau. There comes an old man, and his three sons,——

Cel. I could match this beginning with an old tale.

Le Beau. Three proper young men, of excellent growth and presence;——

Ros. With bills on their necks,—*Be it known unto all men by these presents,*——

Le Beau. The eldest of the three wrestled with Charles, the duke's wrestler; which Charles in a moment threw him, and broke three of his ribs, that there is little hope of life in him: so he served the second, and so the third: Yonder they lie; the poor old man, their father, making such pitiful dole over them, that all the beholders take his part with weeping.

Ros. Alas!

Touch. But what is the sport, monsieur, that the ladies have lost?

Le Beau. Why, this that I speak of.

Touch. Thus men may grow wiser every day! it is the first time that ever I heard, breaking of ribs was sport for ladies.

Cel. Or I, I promise thee.

Ros. But is there ~~any else longs to see this broken music in his sides? is there~~ yet another dotes upon rib-breaking?—Shall we see this wrestling, cousin?

Le Beau. You must, if you stay here: for here is the

place appointed for the wrestling, and they are ready to perform it.

Cel. Yonder, sure, they are coming: Let us now stay and see it.

~~*Flourish.*~~ *Enter Duke* FREDERICK, *Lords,* ORLANDO, CHARLES, *and attendants.*

Duke F. Come on; since the youth will not be entreated, his own peril on his forwardness.

Ros. Is yonder the man?

Le Beau. Even he, madam.

Cel. Alas, he is too young: yet he looks successfully.

Duke F. How now, daughter, and cousin? are you crept hither to see the wrestling?

Ros. Ay, my liege; so please you give us leave.

Duke F. You will take little delight in it, I can tell you, there is such odds in the men: In pity of the challenger's youth, I would fain dissuade him, but he will not be entreated: Speak to him, ladies; see if you can move him.

Cel. Call him hither, good Monsieur Le Beau.

Duke F. Do so; I'll not be by.   [*Duke goes apart.*

Le Beau. Monsieur the challenger, the princesses call for you.

Orl. I attend them, with all respect and duty.

Ros. Young man, have you challenged Charles the wrestler?

Orl. No, fair princess; he is the general challenger: I come but in, as others do, to try with him the strength of my youth.

Cel. Young gentleman, your spirits are too bold for your years: You have seen cruel proof of this man's

ENTER DUKE FREDERICK, LORDS. The names Louis and Eustace for the Duke's first and second lords were invented by John Kemble. (Macready did not print these names in his playbill.) * * * The crowd attending the wrestling match was indeed as numerous as Shepherd's drawing indicates: in Willmott's prompt-book there is a list of all the actors, actresses, and supers in the order of their coming, from which I compute there were seventy-four persons on the stage.

/ Groups of courtiers and Ladies, enter up the terrace steps, and move upon the Scene, as if awaiting the wrestling, - Attendants enter, at the same place, and begin to place chairs, - and prepare the "ring" with ropes and pillars, - As the courtiers catch sight of Celia - or - Rosalind, they respectfully salute them. - When Duke F. enters, with his Suite, - Rosal' - Celia, - &c, retire to R·2 Ent, - where the Attendants are placing seats, - Many of the courtiers - Ladies, - &c, are crowding round Charles, as if congratulating him, - he being, apparently, full of confidence, - other courtiers are talking together, all in high glee, regarding Charles, and occasionally glancing sneeringly at Orlando, who stands modestly apart, at back, by L·3 E, - speaking to Dennis. - The "ring" is formed, as rapidly as possible, but the four entrances to it are not yet closed, - the court being grouped without and within the circle. - The Duke, - Le Beau, - and 2 or 3 of the courtiers, have Merlins on their wrists. |

THE BIRDS AND THE RING. Professor Sprague traces back to 1885 a "bit of antiquarianism" whereby Le Beau carried a live falcon on his wrist (*Shakespeare and the Actors*, p. 32); in this production, whether alive or not, "merlins" were borne by Le Beau, the Duke, and two or three of the courtiers. * * * The setting up of a "professional" wrestling ring of ropes and posts was widely commented on, and was specified by the *Times* reviewer as a "new effect." Sprague's notes on later productions indicate that it started a tradition.

THE WRESTLING MATCH. James Anderson, the Orlando of the play, was proud of the athletic proficiency which he brought to the stage. "Even the wrestling match before the Duke (usually done in the most slovenly manner) aroused the people in the pit to such enthusiasm that they indignantly demanded that the persons on the stage should not stand in front of the ropes of the arena to prevent their seeing the wrestlers. Here my knowledge of the art was very useful. I had a rare good fellow for the champion wrestler Charles, Mr. Mat Howell, whom I taught to wrestle in the Cornish fashion. It was "awfully real," everybody said; but, as I had Mat well padded, there was no fear, on my part, of breaking any of his limbs when he came to earth with a tremendous back fall. The bout was always received with strenuous efforts for an encore, which was never complied with, I need not say" (*An Actor's Life*, p. 113).

Q / The Duke and others that are within the ring, begin to tease it. /

⊙ / As the Duke moves down to his seat, R-2 C,- the Attendants clear and close the ring, - all arrange themselves, without, around the circle . /

Q / takes off his cloak, and gives it to Dennis, at back, R.- /

strength : ~~if you saw yourself with your eyes, or knew yourself with your judgment, the fear of your adventure would counsel you to a more equal enterprise.~~ We pray you, for your own sake, to embrace your own safety, and give over this attempt.

Ros. Do, young sir; your reputation shall not therefore be misprised : we will make it our suit to the duke, that the wrestling might not go forward.

Orl. I beseech you, punish me not with your hard thoughts; wherein I confess me much guilty, to deny so fair and excellent ladies any thing. But let your fair eyes, and gentle wishes, go with me to my trial: wherein if I be foiled, there is but one shamed that was never gracious; if killed, but one dead that is willing to be so: I shall do my friends no wrong, for I have none to lament me; the world no injury, for in it I have nothing; only in the world I fill up a place, which may be better supplied when I have made it empty.

Ros. The little strength that I have, I would it were with you.

Cel. And mine, to eke out hers.

Ros. Fare you well. Pray heaven, I be deceived in you!

Cel. Your heart's desires be with you.

Cha. Come, where is this young gallant, that is so desirous to lie with his mother earth?

Orl. Ready, sir; but his will hath in it a more modest working.

Duke F. You shall try but one fall.

Cha. No, I warrant your grace; you shall not entreat him to a second, that have so mightily persuaded him from a first.

Orl. You mean to mock me after; you should not have mocked me before: but come your ways. Ⓠ

Ros. Now, Hercules be thy speed, young man!

Cel. I would I were invisible, to catch the strong fellow by the leg.   [CHARLES *and* ORLANDO *wrestle.*

Ros. O excellent young man!

Cel. If I had a thunderbolt in mine eye, I can tell who should down.   [CHARLES *is thrown.* ⊙*Shout.*

Duke F. No more, no more.

Orl. Yes, I beseech your grace; I am not yet well breathed.

Duke F. How dost thou, Charles?

Le Beau. He cannot speak, my lord. /*L- of Charles.*/

Duke F. Bear him away.   [CHARLES *is borne out.*

What is thy name, young man?

L- *Orl.* Orlando, my liege; the youngest son of sir Rowland de Bois.

Duke F. I would, thou hadst been son to some man else.

The world esteem'd thy father honourable, ①

But I did find him still mine enemy:

Thou shouldst have better pleas'd me with this deed,

Hadst thou descended from another house.

But fare thee well; thou art a gallant youth;

I would thou hadst told me of another father.

R·21 B - Ac - [*Exeunt Duke* FRED. *Train, and* LE BEAU.

~~*Cel.* Were I my father, coz, would I do this?~~

Orl. I am more proud to be sir Rowland's son,

His youngest son;—and would not change that calling,

To be adopted heir to Frederick. ⊖

Cel.- Were I my father, coz, would I do this?

in the Guards - such preceding him.

LE BEAU. The line "He cannot speak, my lord" had long since been appropriated by stage Touchstones, who sometimes corrupted it and often accompanied it with vaunting antics (*Shakespeare and the Actors*, p. 33). Macready restored the line to Le Beau.

Ø / Great anxiety and interest exhibited by the bye-standers, as the wrestling commences, with cries of encouragement - fear, &c, commencing in a whisper, and as Chas' & Orl' close for the final struggle, the excitement is most intense, and the shoutings loud and vehement

◉ / A general Shout and Applause from all on the Stage. - As the Duke rises, the Attendants - on his signal - take up the pillars, ropes, &c - and exit down terrace steps L.C. - the Courtiers, &c, crowd round in eager congratulation, to Orl' - and give way to the Duke, when Orl' is addressed by him)

① / The Courtiers, &c, become grave, and regard the Duke and Orl' with doubtful and timid glances. - They exeunt diversely, - some following Duke, R-U.C, - others L-U.C, - others, the terrace steps - and all appear to be speaks of Orlando. |

⊖ / goes up L, to Dennis, - who assists him on with his cloak, - cap, &c Dennis afterwards goes off, down terrace steps. |

GEORGE ELLIS. Our artist-scribe, who also played Dennis, made enough of this moment to win a line of notice in the *Examiner*: "Trivial and silent as it was, it was a piece of truth as good as the loud excitement round the wrestlers, when the servant who bore Orlando's cloak, unmoved by the desertion of the court crew, showed such officious kindness and bustling pride in his young master's victory."

Ø / advᵗ to Grl. /

⊙ / he kneels, as she places it on his neck. /

⊖ / Ros' and bel' go towards R-3 b. - /

⨁ / Up turret steps, R-3 b, - Ros' looks back at Grl' as she disappears. /

Ros. My father lov'd sir Rowland as his soul,
And all the world was of my father's mind :
Had I before known this young man his son,
I should have given him tears unto entreaties,
Ere he should thus have ventur'd.
    Cel. Gentle cousin,
Let us go thank him, and encourage him :
My father's rough and envious disposition
Sticks me at heart.—Sir, you have well deserv'd :
If you do keep your promises in love,
But justly, as you have exceeded promise,
Your mistress shall be happy.
    Ros. Gentleman, [*Giving him a chain from her neck.*
Wear this for me ; one out of suits with fortune ;
That could give more, but that her hand lacks means.—
Shall we go, coz ?
    Cel. Ay :—Fare you well, fair gentleman.
    Orl. Can I not say, I thank you ? ~~My better parts~~
~~Are all thrown down ; and that, which here stands up,~~
~~Is but a quintain, a mere lifeless block.~~

in

    Ros. He calls us back : My pride fell with my for-
                tunes :
I'll ask him what he would :—Did you call, sir ?—
Sir, you have wrestled well, and overthrown
More than your enemies.
    Cel. Will you go, coz ?
    Ros. Have with you :—Fare you well.
                    [*Exeunt* ROSALIND *and* CELIA.
    Orl. What passion hangs these weights upon my
                tongue ?
I cannot speak to her, yet she urg'd conference.

<u>*Re-enter* LÈ BEAU.</u> *R-2LB.-*

O poor Orlando! thou art overthrown;
Or Charles, or something weaker, masters thee.

   Le Beau. Good sir, I do in friendship counsel you
To leave this place: Albeit you have deserv'd
High commendation, true applause, and love;
Yet such is now the duke's condition,
That he misconstrues all that you have done.
The duke is humorous; what he is, indeed,
More suits you to conceive, than me to speak of.

   Orl. I thank you, sir: and, pray you, tell me this;
Which of the two was daughter of the duke,
That here was at the wrestling?

   Le Beau. Neither his daughter, if we judge by man-
      ners;
But yet, indeed, the shorter is his daughter:
The other is daughter to the banish'd duke,
And here detain'd by her usurping uncle,
To keep his daughter company; whose loves
Are dearer than the natural bond of sisters.
But I can tell you, that of late this duke
Hath ta'en displeasure 'gainst his gentle niece;
Grounded upon no other argument,
But that the people praise her for her virtues,
And pity her for her good father's sake;
And, on my life, his malice 'gainst the lady
Will suddenly break forth.—Sir, fare you well;
Hereafter, in a better world than this,
I shall desire more love and knowledge of you.

   Orl. I rest much bounden to you: fare you well!
                                 [*Exit* LE BEAU.

                       3

R-2LB.-)

DUKE FREDERICK : cap blue with red lining and gold coronet; shirt showing red through slashings; surcoat yellow and brown with white fur edging; legs in silver armor; shoes red.
OLD DUKE : cap blue with white lining and gold coronet; collar red; great collar ermine; underdress yellow-brown; front and back panels blue and yellow edged with ermine; legs and shoes gray.

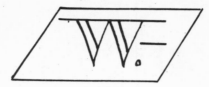

THE STAGING OF I. 3 (140 lines cut to 128). As Orlando went down the Terrace steps, a pair of flats showing "A room in the Palace" closed together in the first grooves.

MY FATHER'S CHILD. Shakespeare's Rosalind is concerned for her "child's father"—i.e., Orlando, whom she thus wittily anticipates she will marry. But this was too indelicate: Macready followed the traditional witless corruption invented by Nicholas Rowe.

Thus must I from the smoke into the smother ;
From tyrant duke, unto a tyrant brother :—
But heavenly Rosalind !   [*Exit, by terrace steps L.*

SCENE III.—*A Room in the Palace.* /1 85./

Enter CELIA *and* ROSALIND, R.

Cel. Why, cousin ; why, Rosalind ;—Cupid have
mercy !—Not a word ?

Ros. Not one to throw at a dog.

Cel. No, thy words are two precious to be cast away
upon curs, throw some of them at me ; come, lame me
with reasons.

Ros. Then there were two cousins laid up ; when the
one should be lamed with reasons, and the other mad
without any.

Cel. But is this all for your father ?

Ros. No, some of it for my child's father: O, how ∧father's child:
full of briars is this working-day world !

Cel. They are but burs, cousin, thrown upon thee in
holiday foolery ; if we walk not in the trodden paths,
our very petticoats will catch them.

Ros. I could shake them off my coat ; these burs are
in my heart.

Cel. Hem them away.

Ros. I would try ; if I could cry hem, and have him.

Cel. Come, come, wrestle with thy affections.

Ros. O, they take the part of a better wrestler than
myself.

Cel. O, a good wish upon you ! you will try in time,
in despite of a fall.—But, turning these jests out of

service, let us talk in good earnest : Is it possible, on such a sudden, you should fall into so strong a liking with old sir Rowland's youngest son?

Ros. The duke my father lov'd his father dearly.

Cel. Doth it therefore ensue, that you should love his son dearly? By this kind of chase, I should hate him, for my father hated his father dearly; yet I hate not Orlando.

Ros. No 'faith, hate him not, for my sake.

Cel. Why should I not? doth he not deserve well?

Ros. Let me love him for that; and do you love him, because I do:—Look, here comes the duke.

Cel. With his eyes full of anger.

Enter Duke FREDERICK, *with* ~~Lords.~~ Eustace, o———

Duke F. Mistress, despatch you with your safest
          haste,
And get you from our court.

Ros. Me, uncle?

Duke F. You, cousin:
Within these ten days if that thou be'st found
So near our publick court as twenty miles,
Thou diest for it.

Ros. I do beseech your grace,
Let me the knowledge of my fault bear with me :
~~If with myself I hold intelligence,~~
Or have acquaintance with mine own desires ;
If that I do not dream, or be not frantick,
~~(As I do trust I am not,) then, dear uncle,~~
Never, so much as in a thought unborn,
Did I offend your highness.

Duke F. Thus do all traitors ;

→ Louis, - and 10 Gentlemen, - R.-

If their purgation did consist in words,
They are as innocent as grace itself:—
Let it suffice thee, that I trust thee not.
 Ros. Yet your mistrust cannot make me a traitor.
Tell me, whereon the likelihood depends.
 Duke F. Thou art thy father's daughter, there's
   enough.
 Ros. So was I, when your highness took his duke-
   dom;
So was I, when your highness banish'd him:
Treason is not inherited, my lord;
Or, if we did derive it from our friends,
What's that to me? my father was no traitor:
Then, good my liege, mistake me not so much,
To think my poverty is treacherous.
 Cel. Dear sovereign, hear me speak.
 Duke F. Ay, Celia; we stay'd her for your sake,
Else had she with her father rang'd along.
 Cel. I did not then entreat to have her stay,
It was your pleasure, and your own remorse;
~~I was too young that time to value her,~~
~~But now I know her~~: if she be a traitor,
Why so am I; we still have slept together,
Rose at an instant, learn'd, play'd, eat together;
And wheresoe'er we went, like Juno's swans,
Still we went coupled, and inseparable.
 Duke F. She is too subtle for thee; and her smooth-
   ness,
Her very silence, and her patience,
Speak to the people, and they pity her.
~~Thou art a fool: she robs thee of thy name;~~

And thou wilt show more bright, and seem more vir-
                    tuous,
When she is gone: then open not thy lips;
Firm and irrevocable is my doom,
Which I have pass'd upon her; she is banish'd. /✗ ℟-/

 Cel. Pronounce that sentence then on me, my liege;
I cannot live out of her company.

/ at /℔-℟-/ - *Duke F.* You are a fool:—You, niece, provide your-
                    self:
If you out-stay the time, upon mine honour,
And in the greatness of my word, you die.
    [*Exeunt Duke* FREDERICK, *and Lords.* ℟:/

℟-   *Cel.* O my poor Rosalind! whither wilt thou go?
Wilt thou change fathers? I will give thee mine.
I charge thee, be not thou more griev'd than I am.

↓. -   *Ros.* I have more cause.

 Cel. Thou hast not, cousin;
Pr'ythee, be chearful: know'st thou not, the duke
Hath banish'd me his daughter?

 Ros. That he hath not.

 Cel. No? hath not? Rosalind lacks then the love,
Which teacheth thee that thou and I am one:
Shall we be sunder'd? shall we part, sweet girl?
No: let my father seek another heir.
Therefore devise with me, how we may fly,
Whither to go, and what to bear with us:
And do not seek to take your change upon you,
To bear your griefs yourself, and leave me out;
For, by this heaven, now at our sorrows pale,
Say what thou canst, I'll go along with thee.

 Ros. Why, whither shall we go?

 Cel. To seek my uncle.

THREE MOOT LINES. The line "And with a kind of umber smirch my face" was always cut in deference to the actresses' pride in appearance. Presumably Shakespeare's boy-actor, Ned, would not have minded. * * * "Because that I am more than common tall" was nicely apropos to both Macready's Rosalinds, Mrs. Nisbett and Miss Faucit. Vezin marks it "out." * * * "A gallant curtle-ax upon my thigh" had formerly been regarded as indelicate: in the Cumberland and Inchbald acting editions it reads, however unscannably, "by my side." The "curtle-ax" was often misinterpreted as a small ax rather than as a cutlass.

THE PLAYING TIME OF ACT I. The performance began at 7:00 P.M. with an overture from the first movement of Beethoven's Pastoral Symphony. A notation at the head of the first scene in Willmott's prompt-book suggests that the overture lasted eight minutes. The act drop fell at 7:40. The text, having been cut from 620 lines to 581, was, therefore, played in thirty-two minutes, at the rate of about eighteen lines per minute. The act drop stayed down for two minutes to cover the ladies change of costume, and the orchestra filled the entr'acte with another passage from the Pastoral Symphony.

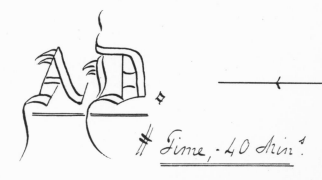

Ros. Alas, what danger will it be to us,
Maids as we are, to travel forth so far?
Beauty provoketh thieves sooner than gold.
    Cel. I'll put myself in poor and mean attire,
~~And with a kind of umber smirch my face;~~
The like do you; so shall we pass along,
And never stir assailants.
    Ros. Were it not better,

but ~~Because that I am more than common tall,~~
That I did suit me all points like a man?
A gallant curtle-ax upon my thigh,
A boar-spear in my hand; and (in my heart
Lie there what hidden woman's fear there will,)
We'll have a swashing and a martial outside;
As many other mannish cowards have,
That do outface it with their semblances.
    Cel. What shall I call thee, when thou art a man?
    Ros. I'll have no worse a name than Jove's own page,
And therefore look you call me, Ganymede.
But what will you be call'd?
    Cel. Something that hath a reference to my state;
No longer Celia, but Aliena.
    Ros. But, cousin, what if we assay'd to steal
The clownish fool out of your father's court?
Would he not be a comfort to our travel?
    Cel. He'll go along o'er the wide world with me;
Leave me alone to woo him: Let's away,
And get our jewels and our wealth together;
Devise the fittest time, and safest way
To hide us from pursuit, that will be made
After my flight: Now go we in content,
To liberty, and not to banishment.   [*Exeunt.* R:/

End Act 1.-

ACT II.

SCENE I.—*The Forest of Arden.*

Enter Duke senior, AMIENS, and other Lords, in the dress of Foresters.

Duke S. Now, my co-mates, and brothers in exíle,
Hath not old custom made this life more sweet
Than that of painted pomp? Are not these woods
More free from peril than the envious court?
Here feel we but the penalty of Adam,
The seasons' difference; as, the icy fang,
And churlish chiding of the winter's wind;
Which when it bites and blows upon my body,
Even till I shrink with cold, I smile, and say,—
This is no flattery: these are counsellors,
That feelingly persuade me what I am.
Sweet are the uses of adversity;
Which, like the toad, ugly and venomous,
Wears yet a precious jewel in his head;
And this our life, exempt from public haunt,
Finds tongues in trees, books in the running brooks,
Sermons in stones, and good in every thing.

Ami. I would not change it: Happy is your grace,
That can translate the stubbornness of fortune
Into so quiet and so sweet a style.

Duke S. Come, shall we go and kill us venison?
And yet it irks me, the poor dappled fools,—

Duke Fred.ᵏ
1ˢᵗ & Lord / Eust. / Louis /
2ⁿᵈ Dᵒ.
8 other Dᵒ.
Adam.
Bag, Staff, Wallet,
2 Bags of money,
Orlando.

Scene 1. - A Room in the palace, - 1ˢᵗ Gro.ˢ

Enter Duke Frederick, - Eustace, - Louis, - and 8 Lords, - L. -

Duke F. /C:/ Can it be possible that no man saw them?
It cannot be: some villains of my court
Are of consent and sufferance in this.

Eustace. /R/ - I cannot hear of any that did see her.
The ladies, her attendants of her chamber,
Saw her a-bed; and in the morning early,
They found the bed untreasur'd of their mistress.

Louis. - /L:/ My lord, the roynish clown, at whom so oft
Your grace was wont &c —————— /Turn over to ⊗ /

THE STAGING OF II. 1 (Folio, II. 2) (21 lines). The act drop rose on the same palace room flats in the first grooves which we had seen at the end of Act I. The traditional staging of the scenes of this act had been in the hodge-podge order of 3, 1, 2, 5, 4, 6, 7. Macready restored it to 2, 3, 1, 4, 5, 6, 7. The one displacement is slightly disturbing to Shakespeare's narrative arrangement, to be played on a non-scenic stage. But on Macready's scenic stage it was clearly more effective to repeat and dispose of the palace and orchard scenes (2 and 3) before revealing the deep beauties of the Forest of Arden (1) and the swirl of forest-scene changes that follow (4, 5, 6, 7). The choice was aesthetic, not merely expeditious.

⊘ /Louis X'es to R:/

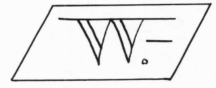

⊙ Girl enters R,- and X'g over to L-2 E,- knocks and calls.

∧ /Ent'g at door, L-2 E,-/

THE STAGING OF II. 2 (Folio, II. 3) (76 lines cut to 73). The palace room flats drew off to reveal the orchard flats in the second grooves, with wings in the first grooves and the house in the second entrance left, exactly as in I. 1.

Your grace was wont to laugh, is also missing.
Hesperia, the princess' gentlewoman,
Confesses, that she secretly o'erheard
Your daughter and her cousin much commend
The parts and graces of the wrestler,
That did but lately foil the sinewy Charles;
And she believes, wherever they are gone,
That youth is surely in their company.

   Duke F. Send to his brother; fetch that gallant
        hither;
If he be absent, bring his brother to me,
I'll make him find him: do this suddenly;
And let not search and inquisition quail
To bring again these foolish runaways.   [*Exeunt.* R:-

SCENE II.—*Before Oliver's House.* / As Sc 1, -Act 1.- /

   Enter ORLANDO *and Adam, meeting.*

  Orl. Who's there?
  Adam. What! my young master?—O, my gentle
     master,
O, my sweet master, O you memory
Of old sir Rowland! why, what make you here?
Why are you virtuous? Why do people love you?
And wherefore are you gentle, strong, and valiant?
Why would you be so fond to overcome
The bony priser of the humourous duke?
Your praise is come too swiftly home before you.
Know you not, master, to some kind of men
Your graces serve them but as enemies?
No more do yours; your virtues, gentle master,

Are sanctified and holy traitors to you.
O, what a world is this, when what is comely
Envenoms him that bears it !
 Orl. Why, what's the matter ?
 Adam. O unhappy youth,
Come not within these doors ; within this roof
The enemy of all your graces lives :
Your brother—(~~no, no brother ; yet the son—~~
~~Yet not the son ;   I will not call him son~~
~~Of him I was about to call his father,~~)
Hath heard your praises ; and this night he means
To burn the lodging where you use to lie,
And you within it : if he fail of that,
He will have other means to cut you off :
I overheard him, and his practices.
This is no place, this house is but a butchery ;
Abhor it, fear it, do not enter it.
 Orl. Why, whither, Adam, would'st thou have me
   go ?
 Adam. No matter whither, so you come not here.
 Orl. What, would'st thou have me go and beg my
   food ?
Or, with a base and boisterous sword, enforce
A thievish living on the common road ?
This I must do, or know not what to do :
Yet this I will not do, do how I can ;
I rather will subjéct me to the malice
Of a diverted blood, and bloody brother.
 Adam. But do not so : I have five hundred crowns,
The thrifty hire I sav'd under your father,
Which I did store, to be my foster-nurse,
When service should in my old limbs lie lame,

2.

Duke Sen:. (Spear)
Amiens.
1st Forest Lord.
2nd Do -
20 other Do.
6 Hunters (Horns.)
12 Attendants

(Spears - Cross and Long Bows,
Quivers. &c)

(Spears, - Hawk frames, and rests, - Dogs,
leash'd together, - &c)

∧ |Adam goes into house, L-2 E, - and brings out bag of money.|

∅ Crl' Exit's R, - Adam re-enters house, and immediately returns with staff, - cap, - and wallet.

And unregarded age in corners thrown;
Take that: and He, that doth the ravens feed,
Yea, providently caters for the sparrow,
Be comfort to my age! Here is the gold;
All this I give you: Let me be your servant;
Though I look old, yet I am strong and lusty:
For in my youth I never did apply
Hot and rebellious liquors in my blood;
Nor did not with unbashful forehead woo
The means of weakness and debility;
Therefore my age is as a lusty winter,
Frosty, but kindly: let me go with you;
I'll do the service of a younger man
In all your business and necessities.

   Orl. O good old man, how well in thee appears
The constant service of the antique world,
When service sweat for duty, not for meed!
Thou art not for the fashion of these times,
Where none will sweat, but for promotion;
And having that, do choke their service up
Even with the having: it is not so with thee.
But, poor old man, thou prun'st a rotten tree,
That cannot so much as a blossom yield,
In lieu of all thy pains and husbandry:
But come thy ways, we'll go along together;
And ere we have thy youthful wages spent,
We'll light upon some settled low content.

   Adam. Master, go on; and I will follow thee,
To the last gasp, with truth and loyalty.—
From seventeen years till now, almost fourscore,
Here lived I, but now live here no more.
At seventeen years many their fortunes seek;

3

But at fourscore, it is too late a week:
Yet fortune cannot recompense me better,
Than to die well, and not my master's debtor.

[*Exeunt.* *R:/*]

3.

SCENE ~~IV~~ *3^{id}*.—*The Forest of Arden, and Duke's* —

Enter ~~RosALIND *in boy's clothes*, CELIA *drest like a*~~
Shepherdess, and TOUCHSTONE.

Ros. O Jupiter! how weary are my spirits!

Touch. I care not for my spirits, if my legs were not weary.

Ros. I could find in my heart to disgrace my man's apparel, and to cry like a woman: but I must comfort the weaker vessel, as doublet and hose ought to shew itself courageous to petticoat: therefore, courage, good Aliena.

Cel. I pray you, bear with me; I cannot go no further.

Touch. For my part, I had rather bear with you, than bear you: yet I should bear no cross, if I did bear you; for, I think, you have no money in your purse.

Ros. Well, this is the forest of Arden.

Touch. Ay, now am I in Arden: the more fool I; when I was at home, I was in a better place; but travellers must be content.

Ros. Ay, be so, good Touchstone:—Look you, who comes here; a young man, and an old, in solemn talk.

Cave /3 & 4 Gr./ - The Duke's Cave, is at the side, L-3 E.-

Six Hunters with their corr de chasse, disc'd L E, - playing a hunting air on their horns. - Attendants are also disc'd variously employed, preparing for the chase, - arranging their cross bows - examining their spears. - &c - Falconers, &c. disc'd with hoops of birds, pass over the stage, and exit L - Hunters Attend'ts lead hounds leash'd to-gether, from the cave, L, - and off, R -1 E, - then enter. several Lords, in the dress of Foresters, preceding the Duke, Senior, and Amiens, similarly dressed, from cave.

Duke S. - Now, my co-mates, and brothers in exile,
Hath not old custom made this life more sweet,
Than that of painted pomp? - Are not these woods
More free from peril than the envious court?
Here feel we but the penalty of Adam,
The seasons' difference; as, the icy fang,
And churlish chiding of the winter's wind;
Which when it bites and blows upon my body,
Even till I shrink with cold, I smile, and say, -
This is no flattery: these are counsellors
That feelingly persuade me what I am.
Sweet are the uses of adversity;
Which, like the toad, ugly and venomous,

3.-

Rosalind.
/Boar Spear./
Celia
/Sheph'd Crook./
Touchstone.
Staff - Wallet, and
Package.
Corin /Sheph'd Crook./
Sylvius. /Pipe &c./

Hear yet a precious jewel in his head;
And this our life, exempt from public haunt,
Finds tongues in trees, books in the running brooks,
Sermons in stones, and good in every thing.

<u>Amiens</u> /R./ I would not change it: Happy is your grace,
That can translate the stubbornness of fortune
Into so quiet and so sweet a style.

<u>Duke S.</u> - Come, shall we go and kill us venison? /going up R.-/
And yet it irks me, the poor dappled fools, —
Being native f–c o_____

THE STAGING OF II. 3 (Folio, II. 1) (69 lines cut to 66). The orchard scene drew off to reveal Duke Senior's company in the Forest of Arden. Forest flats were set in the fourth grooves, and forest wings or "cut flats" in the third grooves. The Duke's Cave at the third entrance left was probably a three-dimensional set piece. Over forty actors appeared—hunters playing on their *cors de chasse*, and attendants readying weapons, leading across the stage braces of hounds, or bearing hoops of falcons. A troop of twenty-two lords dressed as foresters emerged from the cave-mouth, followed by the Duke and Amiens.

RESTORATION OF FIRST LORD. Ever since Charles Johnson's mad mélange of this play and other Shakespearean materials in a comedy called *Love in a Forest* (1723), the First Lord's description of Jaques had been warped into a speech to be given by Jaques himself. The restoration Macready here makes is one of his most significant. But the corruption had become so settled that mere theatre folk of the time took Macready's correction to be a corruption! In his transcription of the "Drury Lane Prompt Bk, London 1842" (New York Public Library), John Moore inserted the following ill-spelled note: "Mr. Macready gave all of Jacques previous to Act 2. Sce. 5 to 1st Lord. Merely I suppose to get Mr. Phelphs into the cast. I have kept the lines for Jacques." This is confusion compounded: the First Lord was played by Elton – Phelps played Adam.

Being native burghers of this desert city,—
Should, in their own confínes, with forked heads
Have their round haunches gor'd.

    1 *Lord.* Indeed, my lord,
The melancholy Jaques grieves at that;
And, in that kind, swears you do more usurp
Than doth your brother, that hath banish'd you.
To-day, my lord of Amiens, and myself,
Did steal behind him, as he lay along
Under an oak, whose antique root peeps out
Upon the brook that brawls along this wood:
To the which place a poor sequester'd stag,
That from the hunters' aim had ta'en a hurt,
Did come to languish; and, indeed, my lord,
The wretched animal heav'd forth such groans,
That their discharge did stretch his leathern coat
Almost to bursting; and the big round tears
Cours'd one another down his innocent nose
In piteous chase: and thus the hairy fool,
~~Much marked of the melancholy Jaques,~~
Stood on the extremest verge of the swift brook,
Augmenting it with tears.

    Duke S. But what said Jaques?
Did he not moralize this spectacle?

    1 *Lord.* O, yes, into a thousand similes.
First, for his weeping in the needless stream;
Poor deer, quoth he, *thou mak'st a testament*
As worldlings do, giving thy sum of more
To that which had too much: Then, being alone,
Left and abandon'd of his velvet friends;
'Tis right, quoth he; *this misery doth part*
The flux of company: Anon, a careless herd,

Full of the pasture, jumps along by him,
And never stays to greet him ; *Ay,* quoth Jaques,
Sweep on, you fat and greasy citizens;
'Tis just the fashion : Wherefore do you look
Upon that poor and broken bankrupt there ?
Thus most invectively he pierceth through
The body of the country, city, court,
Yea, and of this our life : swearing, that we
Are mere usurpers, tyrants, and what's worse,
To fright the animals, and to kill them up,
In their assign'd and native dwelling place.

Duke S. And did you leave him in this contemplation ?
2 Lord. We did, my lord, weeping and commenting
Upon the sobbing deer.

Duke S. Show me the place ;
I love to cope him in these sullen fits,
For then he's full of matter.

1 Lord. I'll bring you to him straight.   [*Exeunt.*

SCENE II.—*A Room in the Palace.*

Enter Duke FREDERICK, *Lords, and Attendants.*

Duke F. Can it be possible, that no man saw them ?
It cannot be : some villains of my court
Are of consent and sufferance in this.

1 Lord. I cannot hear of any that did see her.
The ladies, her attendants of her chamber,
Saw her a-bed ; and, in the morning early,
They found the bed untreasur'd of their mistress.

2 Lord. My lord, the roynish clown, at whom so oft

THE STAGING OF II. 4 (100 lines cut to 87). Forest flats, showing a large tree to the right of center, closed together in the second grooves, with forest wings in the first grooves, and "banks of earth" were thrust on at right and left. These banks of earth were practical set pieces.

Scene 4ᵗʰ - The Forest of Arden - / 1 ∮ 2 ℈ᵣ. /

Enter R-2℮, firstly, Rosalind, in boy's clothes, and with a boar spear, in her hand, - Celia following, dressed like a Shepherdess, and carrying a crook - Touchstone last, with a heavy well filled wallet, and carrying a large canvas package, on his shoulder. - Ros' goes to a tree R, - Celia walks very feebly, to L - Touch' is ℮.-

Ros. - O Jupiter! - how weary are my spirits!

Touch.- I care not for my spirits, if my legs were not weary.

Ros. - I could find in my heart to disgrace my man's apparel, and to
cry like a woman: but I must comfort the weaker vessel, as
doublet and hose ought to shew itself courageous to petticoat:
therefore, / ✗'g to ℮el. / courage, good Aliena.

℮el. - I pray you, bear with me; I can go no further.

Touch.- For my part, I had rather bear with you, than bear you.

Ros. - / look J about. / Well, this is the forest of Arden.

Touch. - Ay, now am I in Arden: the more fool I; when I was
    at home, I was in a better place; but travellers must
    be content.

Ros. - Ay, be so, good Touch-tone: - Look you, who comes
    here; / pointing off L, - / a young man, and an old,
    in solemn talk. o————————————————

Q / Throws himself on a bank of earth, R, - despondingly - Corin, - as tho'
consoling him, goes and sits at his side. /

$\underline{\underline{4}}$.

   [Jaques. / Act. /

    Amiens.

  o 2nd For.t Lord.
    // other Do } , / 2d. /
    4 Attendants.]

2.-   /.-

Enter CORIN *and* SILVIUS. *L.-*

Cor. That is the way to make her scorn you still.

Sil. O Corin, that thou knew'st how I do love her!

Cor. I partly guess; for I have lov'd ere now.

Sil. No, Corin, being old, thou canst not guess;

~~Though in thy youth thou wast as true a lover~~
As ever sigh'd upon a midnight pillow:
But if thy love were ever like to mine,
(As sure I think did never man love so,)

How many actions most ridiculous
Hast thou been drawn to by thy fantasy?

Cor. Into a thousand, that I have forgotten.

Sil. O, thou didst then ne'er love so heartily:
If thou remember'st not the slightest folly,
That ever love did make thee run into,
Thou hast not lov'd:
Or if thou hast not sat as I do now,
Wearying thy hearer in thy mistress' praise,
Thou hast not lov'd:
Or if thou hast not broke from company, /rues./
Abruptly, as my passion now makes me,
Thou hast not lov'd: O Phebe, Phebe, Phebe!

[*Exit* SILVIUS. *R.-/*

Ros. Alas, poor shepherd! searching of thy wound,
I have by hard adventure found mine own.

Touch. And I mine: I remember, when I was in
love, I broke my sword upon a stone, and bid him take
that for coming anight to Jane Smile: and I remember the kissing of her batlet, and then the cow's dugs
that her pretty chop'd hands had milk'd: and I remember the wooing of a peascod instead of her; ~~from~~

~~whom I took two cods, and, giving her them again,~~
~~said with weeping tears, *Wear these for my sake*~~. We,
that are true lovers, run into strange capers ; but as all
is mortal in nature, so is all nature in love mortal in
folly.

Ros. Thou speak'st wiser, than thou art 'ware of.

Touch. Nay, I shall ne'er be 'ware of mine own wit,
till I break my shins against it.

~~*Ros.* Jove! Jove! this shepherd's passion~~
Is much upon my fashion.
Touch. And mine ; but it grows something stale with
~~me.~~

Cel. I pray you, one of you question yond man,
If he for gold will give us any food ;
I faint almost to death.

Touch. Holla ; you, clown !

Ros. Peace, fool ; he's not thy kinsman.

Cor. Who calls ?

Touch. Your betters, sir.

Cor. Else are they very wretched.

Ros. Peace, I say :—
Good even to you, friend. /✗ *to him*./

Cor. And to you, gentle sir, and to you all.

Ros. I pr'ythee, shepherd, if that love, or gold,
Can in this desert place buy entertainment,
Bring us where we may rest ourselves, and feed :
Here's a young maid with travel much oppress'd,
And faints for succour.

Cor. Fair sir, I pity her,
And wish for her sake, more than for mine own,
My fortunes were more able to relieve her :
But I am shepherd to another man,

/ Ros' supports Celia, who leans, also, upon Corin, - Touch' takes up the packages, and follows. /

THE STAGING OF II. 5 (65 lines cut to 61). Rosalind's forest flats and the banks of earth drew off to reveal "Another part of the Forest of Arden," set about with tables and stools "under the shade of a large tree." (See Ellis's sketch). The wings and flats, including cut flats, were set in the third, fourth, and fifth grooves. Some eighteen persons were lounging about, listening to Amiens's song, and preparing the Duke's banquet. It was doubtless this scene that R. H. Horne remembered so vividly in after years: "The Forest of Arden, where the romantic Duke had taken up his abode, was represented [as his] rustic palace, with an entire covering of tangled boughs and foliage high overhead, among the leaves of which, with the delicate tints, peeps of sky, and glancing green lights, there was a constant moving and fluttering, as of soft winds and small birds, whose sweet warbling fitfully blended with the subdued strains of the orchestra below." (*Contemporary Review*, October, 1871).

And do not sheer the fleeces that I graze;
My master is of churlish disposition,
~~And little reeks to find the way to heaven~~
~~By doing deeds of hospitality:~~
Besides, his cote, his flocks, and bounds of feed,
Are now on sale, and at our sheepcote now,
By reason of his absence, there is nothing
That you will feed on; but what is, come see,
And in my voice most welcome shall you be. /×ℒ.-/

 Ros. What is he, that shall buy his flock and pasture?
 Cor. That young swain that you saw here but ere-
    while,
That little cares for buying any thing.
 Ros. I pray thee, if it stand with honesty,
Buy thou the cottage, pasture, and the flock,
And thou shalt have to pay for it of us.
 Cel. And we will mend thy wages: I like this place,
And willingly could waste my time in it.
 Cor. Assuredly, the thing is to be sold:
Go with me; if you like, upon report,
The soil, the profit, and this kind of life,
I will your very faithful feeder be,
And buy it with your gold right suddenly.   [*Exeunt.* ℒ.-/ ⊘

SCENE V.—*The same.*
/Another part of the Forest of Arden./ 3-ℒ. f-5 g.ᵒ./
~~Enter~~ AMIENS, JAQUES, and others, *dis.ᵈ*

SONG.

 Ami. Under the greenwood tree,
  Who loves to lie with me,

> *And tune his merry note*
> *Unto the sweet bird's throat,*
> *Come hither, come hither, come hither;*
> *Here shall he see*
> *No enemy,*
> *But winter and rough weather.*

Jaq. More, more, I pr'ythee, more.

Ami. It will make you melancholy, monsieur Jaques.

Jaq. I thank it. More, I pr'ythee, more. I can suck melancholy out of a song, as a weazel sucks eggs; More, I pr'ythee, more.

Ami. My voice is ragged; I know, I cannot please you.

Jaq. I do not desire you to please me, I do desire you to sing: Come, more; another stanza; Call you them stanzas?

Ami. What you will, monsieur Jaques.

Jaq. Nay, I care not for their names; they owe me nothing: Will you sing?

Ami. More at your request, than to please myself.

Jaq. Well then, if ever I thank any man, I'll thank you: but that they call compliment, is like the encounter of two dog-apes; and when a man thanks me heartily, methinks, I have given him a penny, and he renders me the beggarly thanks. Come, sing; and you, that will not, hold your tongues.

Ami. Well, I'll end the song.—Sirs, cover the while; the duke will drink under this tree:—he hath been all this day to look you.

Jaq. And I have been all this day to avoid him. He is too dispútable for my company: I think of as

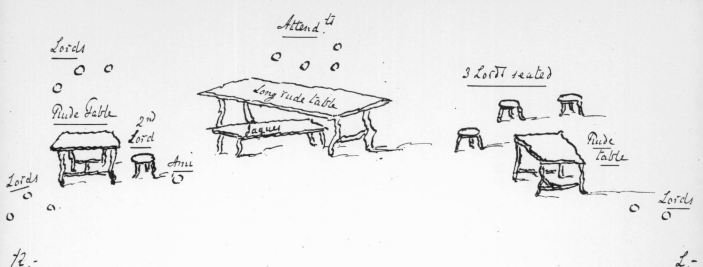

Lords

Attend.^ts

3 Lords seated

Rude Table

2nd Lord

Long rude table

Jaques

Rude Table

Ami.

Lords

Lords

Lords

R.-   L.-

The C.-Table is set under the shade of a large tree, - Attendants are busy arranging seats for the Duke's repast, - Rude seats - benches and stools - in confusion about the Scene. - Wooden dishes, - flagons, - and casks, laid about. - Several Lords disc^d - some seated, - others lying on the ground. - Jaques is stretched, at full length, on C bench. - Spears, - Bows - Quivers, &c strewn in various places.

⊘ / To the Attendants, who have previously been listening to the song, - they exit R - 2L C. - /

RESTORATION. Traditionally Amiens's song had been cut to a single stanza and Jaques's parody of it omitted; the scene had been padded with lines for Jaques lifted from the fourth act and had been generally disarranged. Macready restored the scene all but completely and provided it full musical treatment.

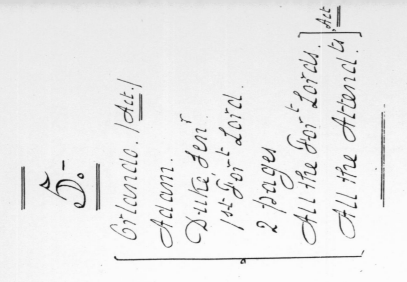

Ø /Jaques rises, and act.s C, - with the others. /

DUCDAME. Insisting that this be pronounced "Duc-ad-me," Macready was following Thomas Hanmer's effort (1743–44) to make dog-Latin sense of it.

⊘ / pronounced - ducadme. /

⊖ / The Attendants re-enter here, R. & L. C, - with the stands, which they place on the tables. /

5.

many matters as he ; but I give heaven thanks, and make no boast of them.   Come, warble, come.

— *Quartette*. — ~~SONG~~. /*Amiens & 3 Lords.*/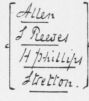

    Who doth ambition shun,   [All together here.
    And loves to live i'the sun,
    Seeking the food he eats,
    And pleas'd with what he gets,
Come hither, come hither, come hither ;
        Here shall he see
        No enemy,
But winter and rough weather. ⊘

Jaq. I'll give you a verse to this note, that I made yesterday in despite of my invention.
Ami. And I'll sing it.
Jaq. Thus it goes :

    If it do come to pass,
    That any man turn ass,
    Leaving his wealth and ease,
    A stubborn will to please,
Ducdàme, ducdàme, ducdàme ;
        Here shall he see,
        Gross fools as he,
An if he will come to Ami. — /*going L:*/

Ami. What's that *ducdàme?* ⊘
Jaq. 'Tis a Greek invocation, to call fools into a circle. I'll go sleep if I can; if I cannot, I'll rail against all the first-born of Egypt. ⊖ •————→ /*Exit L:*/

Ami. And I'll go seek the duke; his banquet is pre-par'd.   [*Exeunt severally.*

SCENE VI.—*The same.* /1 gr./

Enter ORLANDO *and* ADAM. R.-

Adam. Dear master, I can go no further: O, I die for food! Here lie I down and measure out my grave. Farewell, kind master.

Orl. Why, how now, Adam! no greater heart in thee? Live a little; comfort a little; cheer thyself a little: If this uncouth forest yield any thing savage, I will either be food for it, or bring it for food to thee. Thy conceit is nearer death than thy powers. For my sake, be comfortable; hold death awhile at the arm's end: I will here be with thee presently; and if I bring thee not something to eat, I'll give thee leave to die: but if thou diest before I come, thou art a mocker of my labour. Well said! thou look'st cheerily: and I'll be with thee quickly.—Yet thou liest in the bleak air: Come, I will bear thee to some shelter; and thou shalt not die for lack of a dinner, if there live any thing in this desert. Cheerly, good Adam! —— [*Exeunt.* L:/

SCENE VII.—*The same,* as Sc 5.

A table set out. Enter Duke senior, AMIENS, *Lords,* and all the as Foresters,- R.2LE *and others*.

Duke S. I think he be transform'd into a beast; For I can no where find him like a man.

Q /Goes up with the Lords, as Scene closes in./

THE STAGING OF II. 6 (16 lines). Forest flats closed together in the first grooves for this tiny scene of Adam and Orlando.

THE STAGING OF II. 7 (200 lines cut to 147). The first groove flats drew off to reveal again the Duke's banquet scene exactly as in II. 5, but now populated by the Duke's whole company.

————> ——— The Attend[ts] are dis[d] busy about the table, C, - which is set out with meats, - fruits, - flagons of wine - wine cups, - &c - Seats are placed around the table which is set oblique from R-LL C, - towards 2 Ent. L, - 2 pages in attendance, near the Duke's seat. - Two other tables, - seats, - &c R & L. -

MACREADY'S JAQUES

(*See Frontispiece*)

The critics tended to give only token notice to Macready's Jaques, on the grounds that it was well-known to experienced play-goers. As a matter of fact he had not played it at all for over three years and, according to William Archer's count, had played it in London only twenty times since 1819. Since it was not a leading role it was not particularly serviceable to Macready, and I think he never reverted to it after this 1842–43 season.

Lady Pollock, writing after Macready's death, recalled his Jaques as "somewhat too sombre" to be wholly successful. Yet she claimed for it "many suggestive and excellent passages," especially in his account of the meeting with the fool. "He came on the scene laughing to himself, evidently much diverted with his thoughts; and the interjections of mirth with which he broke his reply to the Duke's observation, 'What! you look merrily!' had a due measure of bitterness in them; while during his pause between 'a motley fool—a miserable world,' the expression of his countenance gave to the passage its true significance, showing his contemptuous pity for humanity which could be so sharply satirized by the common jester." When he quoted Touchstone, she tells us, he gave the words all their meaning yet without resorting to downright mimicry of Touchstone, and "the speech was concluded with a fresh burst of sarcastic merriment, which was in the true spirit of Jaques" (*Macready As I Knew Him*, pp. 134–136).

Of the critics who did notice him on this occasion, their compliments were often somewhat double-edged. The *Athenaeum* thought his personation was "the nearest of any to the true character" and added that he was "more free from the mannerisms of our stage elocution than formerly." *The Times* praised his "All the world's a stage" for being "particularly forcible and free from that overstriving at light and shade which is the prevailing blemish of his acting." *John Bull*, though acknowledging that "no actor appears by nature better fitted to personate this beautiful creation of harmonious inconsistencies," yet dismissed most of the performance as too generalized: "it might have been anybody speaking." Eight months later, however, after the royal command performance, this same critic praised Macready without stint: "He is the best representative we have ever seen of Shakespeare's pensive moralist, of whose 'humorous sadness' he gives a beautiful picture. His delivery of the famous 'All the world's a stage' is admirable. He does not make it, as others do, a piece of emphatic declamation, but speaks it, as it were involuntarily, in a musing manner, and as if he were thinking aloud." The *Spectator*, too, was enchanted by his naturalness: "We never heard Macready deliver a speech with such spontaneous ease as the famous one of the 'seven ages of man': he spoke it as giving utterance to thought suggested at the instant by the foregoing remark of the Duke."

1 *Lord.* My lord, he is but even now gone hence ;
Here was he merry, hearing of a song.
Duke S. If he, compact of jars, grow musical,
We shall have shortly discord in the spheres :—
Go, seek him ; tell him, I would speak with him.

Enter JAQUES. *L.-*

1 *Lord.* He saves my labour by his own approach.
Duke S. Why, how now, monsieur! what a life is
      this,
That your poor friends must woo your company?
What ! you look merrily.
Jaq. A fool, a fool !——I met a fool i' the forest,
A motley fool ;—a miserable world !—
As I do live by food, I met a fool ;
Who laid him down and bask'd him in the sun,
And rail'd on lady Fortune in good terms,
In good set terms,—and yet a motley fool.
Good-morrow, fool, quoth I : *No, sir,* quoth he,
Call me not fool, till heaven hath sent me fortune :
And then he drew a dial from his poke ;
And looking on it with lack-lustre eye,
Says, very wisely, *It is ten o'clock :*
Thus may we see, quoth he, *how the world wags :*
'Tis but an hour ago, since it was nine ;
And after an hour more, 'twill be eleven ;
And so, from hour to hour, we ripe and ripe,
And then, from hour to hour, we rot, and rot,
And thereby hangs a tale. When I did hear
The motley fool thus moral on the time,
My lungs began to crow like chanticleer,
That fools should be so deep-contemplative ;

And I did laugh, sans intermission,
An hour by his dial.—O noble fool!
A worthy fool! Motley's the only wear.   *All go to the table, — and sit.)*

~~Duke S. What fool is this?~~

   Jaq. O worthy fool!—One, that hath been a cour-
      tier;
And says, if ladies be but young, and fair,
They have the gift to know it: and in his brain,—
Which is as dry as the remainder bisket
After a voyage,—he hath strange places cramm'd
With observation, the which he vents
In mangled forms:—O, that I were a fool!
I am ambitious for a motley coat.
   Duke S. Thou shalt have one.
   Jaq. It is my only suit;
Provided, that you weed your better judgments
Of all opinion that grows rank in them,
That I am wise. I must have liberty
Withal, as large a charter as the wind,
To blow on whom I please; for so fools have:
And they, that are most galled with my folly,
They most must laugh: And why, sir, must they so?
The *why* is plain as way to parish church:
He, that a fool doth very wisely hit,
Doth very foolishly, although he smart,
Not to seem senseless of the bob: if not,
The wise man's folly is anatomiz'd
Even by the squand'ring glances of the fool.
Invest me in my motley; give me leave
To speak my mind, and I will through and through
Cleanse the foul body of the infected world,
If they will patiently receive my medicine.

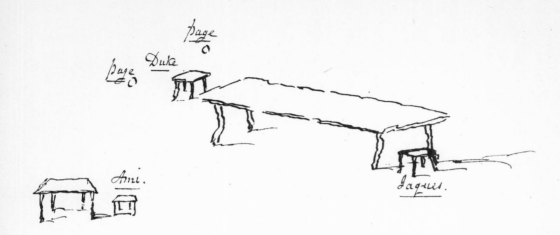

JAQUES EVISCERATED. This enormous excision of what one might call the quintessence of Shakespeare's Jaques was traditional, and regrettably Macready acquiesced in it. Originally, in his own copy, he inked out only the Duke's line, "As sensual as the brutish sting itself," and Jaques's last fifteen lines, but he circled the whole section with pencil, as if mindful of the tradition, and eventually he let it all go. The effect of this is to pull Jaques's teeth. Shorn of his best invective, Macready's Jaques was probably just what his Victorian audience wanted him to be: noble, loving wise, and fatherly tender.

ORLANDO'S ENTRANCE. "All go to the tables and sit" as Orlando breaks in—seemingly an ineffective entrance because upon a "busy" stage. The prompt-books of John Moore (1842 and 1848) and James Taylor improve the entrance as "Through vampire bush on top of bluff RUE"; but no such spectacular leap occurred on Macready's stage.

Duke S. Fye on thee! I can tell what thou wouldst
    do.
  Jaq. What, for a counter, would I do, but good?
  Duke S. Most mischievous foul sin, in chiding sin:
For thou thyself hast been a libertine,
As sensual as the brutish sting itself;
And all the embossed sores, and headed evils,
That thou with license of free foot hast caught,
Wouldst thou disgorge into the general world.
  Jaq. Why, who cries out on pride,
That can therein tax any private party?
Doth it not flow as hugely as the sea,
Till that the very very means do ebb?
What woman in the city do I name,
When that I say, The city-woman bears
The cost of princes on unworthy shoulders?
Who can come in, and say, that I mean her,
When such a one as she, such is her neighbour?
Or what is he of basest function,
That says, his bravery is not on my cost,
(Thinking that I mean him,) but therein suits
His folly to the mettle of my speech?
There then; How, what then? Let me see wherein
My tongue hath wrong'd him: if it do him right,
Then he hath wrong'd himself; if he be free,
Why then, my taxing like a wild goose flies,
Unclaim'd of any man.—But who comes here?

    Enter ORLANDO, *with his sword drawn.*

  Orl. Forbear, and eat no more.
  Jaq. Why, I have eat none yet.
  Orl. Nor shalt not, till necessity be serv'd.

Jaq. Of what kind should this cock come of?

Duke S. Art thou thus bolden'd, man, by thy distress; */All rue./*

Or else a rude despiser of good manners,
That in civility thou seem'st so empty?

Orl. You touch'd my vein at first; the thorny point
Of bare distress hath ta'en from me the show
Of smooth civility : yet am I inland bred,
And know some nurture: But forbear, I say;
He dies, that touches any of this fruit,
Till I and my affairs are answered.

Jaq. An you will not be answered with reason,
I must die.

Duke S. What would you have? your gentleness
shall force,
More than your force move us to gentleness.

Orl. I almost die for food, and let me have it.

Duke S. Sit down and feed, and welcome to our
table.

Orl. Speak you so gently? Pardon me, I pray you :
I thought, that all things had been savage here;
And therefore put I on the countenance
Of stern commandment: But whate'er you are,
That in this desert inaccessible,
Under the shade of melancholy boughs,
Lose and neglect the creeping hours of time;
If ever you have look'd on better days;
If ever been where bells have knoll'd to church;
If ever sat at any good man's feast;
If ever from your eye-lids wip'd a tear,
And know what 'tis to pity, and be pitied;
Let gentleness my strong enforcement be :

JAMES ANDERSON'S ORLANDO

Anderson was a strapping, handsome young actor whom Macready had brought to Covent Garden from the provinces in 1837. Now, at the age of thirty-one, he was serving Macready partly in "leading business" and partly in labors of management. As Orlando he "bears himself gallantly" said the *Athenaeum*, "both in defying his brother and overthrowing the wrestler." *The Times* thought his acting along with Fanny Stirling's the best in the play, praising his "frank and manly bearing," his "affection for Old Adam," and "the ease and good humor of his scenes with the women." *John Bull*, however, scolded him for artificiality of vocal patterns, for failing to deliver an "image of inborn chivalry and manly grace," and, rather oddly, for being a "sentimentalist." One would gather from Anderson's published reminiscences, *An Actor's Life*, written near the end of the century, that as a young man he was on the bullish, slangy, callow side rather than the sentimental. His only particularized recollection of this production was his own prowess in arranging and executing the wrestling match.

∧ /*Comes forward a little.*/

b.‒

Adam.

∧ / Advancing C, – with the others. /

ALL THE WORLD'S A STAGE. It is interesting that Macready did not "take the focus" for this speech. The Duke and others advanced to center and Jaques kept well to the left. Nor, apparently, did he accompany it in "the old way," as Professor Sprague describes the typical Victorian rendition of it, "with a full display of the actor's powers of mimicry" (*Shakespeare and the Actors*, p. 35); rather he spoke it "involuntarily, in a musing manner, and as if he were thinking aloud."

In the which hope, I blush, and hide my sword.

Duke S. True is it that we have seen better days;
And have with holy bell been knoll'd to church;
And sat at good men's feasts; and wip'd our eyes
Of drops, that sacred pity hath engender'd:
And therefore sit you down in gentleness,
And take upon command what help we have,
That to your wanting may be ministred.

Orl. Then, but forbear your food a little while,
Whiles, like a doe, I go to find my fawn,
And give it food.   There is an old poor man,
Who after me hath many a weary step
Limp'd in pure love; till he be first suffic'd,—
Oppress'd with two weak evils, age and hunger,—
I will not touch a bit.

Duke S. Go find him out,
And we will nothing waste till you return.

Orl. I thank ye; and be bless'd for your good com-
            fort!   [*Exit, 𝓛 ·/*

Duke S. Thou seest, we are not all alone unhappy:
This wide and universal theatre
Presents more woeful pageants than the scene,
Wherein we play in.

Jaq. All the world's a stage,
And all the men and women merely players:
They have their exits and their entrances;
And one man in his time plays many parts,
His acts being seven ages.   At first, the infant,
Mewling and puking in the nurse's arms;
And then, the whining school-boy, with his satchel,
And shining morning face, creeping like snail
Unwillingly to school: And then, the lover;

3

Sighing like furnace, with a woeful ballad
Made to his mistress' eye-brow : Then, a soldier ;
Full of strange oaths, and bearded like the pard,
Jealous in honour, sudden and quick in quarrel,
Seeking the bubble reputation
Even in the cannon's mouth : And then, the justice ;
In fair round belly, with good capon lin'd,
With eyes severe, and beard of formal cut,
Full of wise saws and modern instances,
And so he plays his part : The sixth age shifts
Into the lean and slipper'd pantaloon ;
With spectacles on nose, and pouch on side ;
His youthful hose well sav'd, a world too wide
For his shrunk shank ; and his big manly voice,
Turning again toward childish treble, pipes
And whistles in his sound : Last scene of all,
That ends this strange eventful history,
Is second childishness, and mere oblivion ;
Sans teeth, sans eyes, sans taste, sans every thing.

Re-enter ORLANDO, *with* ADAM. *L.-* Q

Duke S. Welcome : Set down your venerable bur-
    den,
And let him feed. ⊙
    Orl. I thank you most for him.
    Adam. So had you need ;
I scarce can speak, to thank you for myself.
    Duke S. Welcome, fall to : I will not trouble you
As yet, to question you about your fortunes :—
Give us some musick ; and, good cousin, sing.

2

Ø / Jaques, j-c, assist Adam, and place him at end of b-table, - his back to the audience. /

◉ / All go up with Duke. /

∧ / All sit. /

∧ /rising, - and coming forward with Grl ! and the others. /

AMIENS *sings.*

SONG.

I.

Blow, blow, thou winter wind,
Thou art not so unkind
   As man's ingratitude;
Thy tooth is not so keen,
Because thou art not seen,
   Although thy breath be rude.
Heigh, ho! sing, heigh, ho! unto the green holly:
Most friendship is feigning, most loving mere folly:
   Then, heigh, ho, the holly!
   This life is most jolly.

Chorus.

II.

Freeze, freeze, thou bitter sky,
That dost not bite so nigh
   As benefits forgot:
Though thou the waters warp,
Thy sting is not so sharp
   As friend remember'd not.
Heigh, ho! sing, heigh, ho! &c.

  Duke S. If that thou were the good sir Rowland's
    son,—
As you have whisper'd faithfully, you were;
And as mine eye doth his effigies witness
Most truly limn'd, and living in your face,—
Be truly welcome hither: I am the duke,

That lov'd your father: The residue of your fortune,
Go to my cave and tell me.—Good old man,
Thou art right welcome as thy master is:
Support him by the arm.—Give me your hand, /to Orl./
And let me all your fortunes understand.   [*Exeunt.*

/R-2L.B.-/

/Music of the Foresters, - played at the opening of Sc 3 - this Act, - heard as the Drop falls. /

—— End of Act 2.——

THE PLAYING TIME OF ACT II. Ellis calls it flatly fifty minutes; Willmott noted the curtain fall as variously between twenty-six and thirty minutes past eight o'clock. The text, cut from 547 lines to 471, is 110 lines shorter than the first act, yet it took some fifteen minutes longer to play. One can only surmise that the two songs in the act were developed into full concert numbers, that the increased number of slidings of scenery cost a minute or two, and that Macready's Jaques spent all the speaking time befitting his dignity. The overall movement of the lines was not more than ten per minute. The act drop remained down some two or three minutes while the orchestra played, to cover Orlando's change to his forester costume.

THE STAGING OF III. 1 (18 lines). The act drop rose again on the palace room flats in the first grooves.

Duke Fred^k. Oliver. Beatrice Louis. 8 court Lords. 2 Attendants. Orlando. W^s papers. N°1. Corin. Touchstone Sheph^s to Book. Shepherd. Pipe. ♯ Sheep Bell ready See prompter.

♯♯ Music of Shepherd's Pipe, - heard, as Scene opens.

ACT III.

SCENE I.—*A Room in the Palace.* / /*fri.* /

Eu-tace Lows.-8   2

Enter Duke FREDERICK, OLIVER, *Lords, and Atten-*
dants, who guard Oliver.   R.-

Duke F. Not see him since? Sir, sir, that cannot be : / *pacing*
But were I not the better part made mercy,   *the*
I should not seek an absent argument   *stage.* /
Of my revenge, thou present : But look to it ;
Find out thy brother, wheresoe'er he is ;
~~Seek him with candle~~ ; bring him dead or living,
Within this twelvemonth, or turn thou no more
To seek a living in our territory.
Thy lands, and all things that thou dost call thine,
Worth seizure, do we seize into our hands ;
Till thou canst quit thee by thy brother's mouth,
Of what we think against thee.

Oli. O, that your highness knew my heart in this !
I never lov'd my brother in my life.

Duke F. More villain thou.—Well, push him out of
            doors ;
And let my officers of such a nature
Make an extent upon his house and lands :
Do this expediently, and turn him going.   [*Exeunt,* R.-

/ - *Oliver being forced off R.-* /

SCENE II.—*The Forest.* 3 4 -5 for. o——
dur reading
~~Enter~~ ORLANDO, ~~with~~ a paper, *which he has,* o

Orl. Hang there, my verse, in witness of my love:
And, thou, thrice-crowned queen of night, survey
With thy chaste eye, from thy pale sphere above,
Thy huntress' name, that my full life doth sway.
O Rosalind! these trees shall be my books,
And in their barks my thoughts I'll character;
That every eye, which in this forest looks,
Shall see thy virtue witness'd every where.
Run, run, Orlando; carve, on every tree,
The fair, the chaste, and unexpressive she.   [*Exit, L.*

Enter CORIN *and* TOUCHSTONE.   12-21 £ -

Cor. And how like you this shepherd's life, master Touchstone?

Touch. Truly, shepherd, in respect of itself, it is a good life; but in respect that it is a shepherd's life, it is naught. In respect that it is solitary, I like it very well; but in respect that it is private, it is a very vile life. ~~Now in respect it is in the fields, it pleaseth me well; but in respect it is not in the court, it is tedious.~~ As it is a spare life, look you, it fits my humour well; but as there is no more plenty in it, it goes much against my stomach. Hast any philosophy in thee, shepherd?

Cor. No more, but that I know, the more one sickens, the worse at ease he is; and that he that wants money, means, and content, is without three

[Summer Evening.]

placed on a tree, at back C. – A Shepherd, also, disc.ᵈ seated on a bank, at
2 H.L, – playing on a pipe, – his back being to the audience.

Tinkling of the
Sheep Bell, heard,
occasionally.

2.-

Rosalind.
Celia.
H.ⁿ Paper, N.º 2.-

THE STAGING OF III. 2 (Folio, III. 2 and 3) (565 lines cut to 458). The palace room flats drew off to reveal forest flats in the fifth groove, forest wings or "cut flats" showing a large tree at center in the third and fourth grooves, and a bank of earth at the second entrance left. In deference to the "thrice-crowned queen of night," Macready intended this as an evening scene, and wrote in his own book "moon seen faintly in the sky" (James Taylor's copy reads "Morning Break of Day.") Seated on the bank a shepherd piped an obbligato to Orlando's love poem, and throughout the scene were heard the tinkling of sheep-bells—an effect that was long remembered. One day in the 1850's Lady Pollock was strolling with Macready outside of Sherborne: "As we were lingering and loitering . . . through a green meadow, silently enjoying the beauty of the country, a flock of startled sheep scrambled over the hedge that skirted the meadow, and the leader's bell tinkling with its delicate tender tone broke the silence. 'Listen to that sound,' said Macready; 'isn't it delicious? I introduced it in *As You Like It*. Ah! that was my favourite production' " (*Macready As I Knew Him*, p. 20).

CUTTING. The thirty-line cut from the Touchstone-Corin dialogue was traditional. But the excision of "the copulation of cattle," etc., in Touchstone's next speech was a purification original with Macready.

good friends :—That the property of rain is to wet, and fire to burn : That good pasture makes fat sheep; and that a great cause of the night, is lack of the sun : That he, that hath learned no wit by nature nor art, may complain of good breeding, or comes of a very dull kindred.

Touch. Such a one is a natural philosopher. Wast. ever in court, shepherd ?

Cor. No, truly.

Touch. Then thou art damn'd.

Cor. Nay, I hope,——

Touch. Truly, thou art damn'd ; like an ill-roasted egg, all on one side.

Cor. For not being at court? Your reason.

Touch. Why, if thou never wast at court, thou never saw'st good manners; if thou never saw'st good manners, then thy manners must be wicked; and wickedness is sin, and sin is damnation : Thou art in a parlous state, shepherd.

Cor. Not a whit, Touchstone: ~~those, that are good manners at the court, are as ridicul~~ous in the country, as the behaviour of the country is most mockable at the court. You told me, you salute not at the court, but you kiss your hands; that courtesy would be uncleanly, if courtiers were shepherds.

Touch. Instance, briefly; come, instance.

Cor. Why, we are still handling our ewes; and their fells, you know, are greasy.

Touch. Why, do not your courtier's hands sweat? and is not the grease of a mutton as wholesome as the sweat of a man? Shallow, shallow: A better instance, I say; come.

Cor. Besides, our hands are hard.

Touch. Your lips will feel them the sooner. Shallow, again : A more sounder instance, come.

Cor. And they are often tarr'd over with the surgery of our sheep ; and would you have us kiss tar? The courtier's hands are perfumed with civet.

Touch. Most shallow man ! Thou worms-meat, in respect of a good piece of flesh : Indeed !—Learn of the wise, and perpend : Civet is of a baser birth than tar ; the very uncleanly flux of a cat. Mend the instance, shepherd.

Cor. You have too courtly a wit for me ; I'll rest.

Touch. Wilt thou rest damn'd ? God help thee, shallow man ! God make incision in thee ! thou art raw.

Cor. Sir, I am a true labourer ; I earn that I eat, get that I wear ; owe no man hate, envy no man's happiness ; glad of other men's good, content with my harm : and the greatest of my pride is, to see my ewes graze, and my lambs suck.

Touch. That is another simple sin in you ; to bring the ewes and the rams together, and to offer to get your living by the copulation of cattle : to be bawd to a bell-wether ; and to betray a she-lamb of a twelve-month, to a crooked-pated, old, cuckoldly ram, out of all reasonable match. If thou be'st not damn'd for this, the devil himself will have no shepherds ; I cannot see else how thou shouldst 'scape. /X ½ .-/

Cor. Here comes young master Ganymede, my new mistress's brother.

Ø /Touch' and Corin go up, - as Rosalind enters R-21 C. - sees paper on C-tree, - takes it off, and reads, as she ads¹. /

ROSALIND : hat black with red and white plume; cape gray; dress blue; cutlass brown; legs rose; shoes black.

CELIA : hair bands gold, red, blue; overdress yellow and lavender on white, with brown collar, cuffs, and bottom edging; sleeves gray; underdress rose and yellow.

Enter ROSALIND, ~~reading a paper.~~   *12 - 21 C. -*

Ros. *From the east to western Ind,*
 No jewel is like Rosalind.
 Her worth, being mounted on the wind,
 Through all the world bears Rosalind.
 All the pictures, fairest lin'd,
 Are but black to Rosalind.
 Let no face be kept in mind,
 But the fair of Rosalind.

Written.
No. 1. -

Touch. I'll rhime you so, eight years together ; din-   *lad'g R*
ners, and suppers, and sleeping hours excepted : It is
the right butter-woman's ~~rank~~ to market.

Ros. Out, fool !   *rate*

Touch. For a taste :———

 If a hart do lack a hind,
 Let him seek out Rosalind.
 If the cat will after kind,
 So, be sure, will Rosalind.
 ~~*Winter-garments must be lin'd,*~~
 So must slender Rosalind.
 They that reap, must sheaf and bind :
 Then to cart with Rosalind.
 Sweetest nut hath sowrest rind,
 Such a nut is Rosalind.
 He that sweetest rose will find,
 Must find love's prick, and Rosalind.

This is the very false gallop of verses ; Why do you
infect yourself with them ?

Ros. Peace, you dull fool ; I found them on a tree.

Touch. Truly, the tree yields bad fruit.

Ros. I'll graff it with you, and then I shall graff it with a medlar : then it will be the earliest fruit in the country : for you'll be rotten e'er you be half ripe, and that's the right virtue of the medlar.

Touch. You have said ; but whether wisely or no, let the forest judge.

     Enter CELIA, *reading a paper.*

Ros. Peace !
Here comes my sister, reading ; stand aside.

 Cel. *Why should this desert silent be ?*
   For it is unpeopled ? No ;
 Tongues I'll hang on every tree,
  That shall civil sayings show.
 Some, how brief the life of man
  Runs his erring pilgrimage ;
 That the stretching of a span
  Buckles in his sum of age.
 Some, of violated vows
  'Twixt the souls of friend and friend :
 But upon the fairest boughs,
  Or at every sentence' end,
 Will I Rosalinda write ;
  Teaching all, that read, to know
 The quintessence of every sprite
  Heaven would in little show.
 Therefore heaven nature charg'd
  That one body should be fill'd
 With all graces wide enlarg'd :
  Nature presently distill'd
 Helen's cheek, but not her heart ;

Written
No 2.

Q / While reading the paper, Celia X'es over to R: /

GENTLE JUPITER. Modern editions usually print "pulpiter." This emendation, by James Spedding, had not yet been suggested.

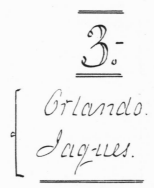

CUTTING. The Pythagoras and Irish rat line, the "South-sea of discovery" and the "man in your belly" line were traditionally omitted.

> *Cleopatra's majesty ;*
> *Atalanta's better part ;*
>   *Sad Lucretia's modesty.*
> ~~*Thus Rosalind of many parts*~~
>   *By heavenly synod was devis'd ;*
> *Of many faces, eyes, and hearts,*
>   *To have the touches dearest priz'd.*
> *Heaven would that she these gifts should have,*
> *And I ~~do~~ live and die her slave.*

Ros. O most gentle Jupiter!—what tedious homily of love have you wearied your parishioners withal, and never cry'd, *Have patience, good people !*

Cel. How now! back friends ;—Shepherd, go off a little :—Go with him, sirrah.

Touch. Come, shepherd, let's make an honourable retreat ; though not with bag and baggage, yet with scrip and scrippage. [*Exeunt* CORIN *and* TOUCHSTONE.

Cel. Didst thou hear these verses ?

Ros. O, yes, I heard them all, and more too ; ~~for some of them had in them more feet than the verses would bear.~~

Cel. That's no matter ; the feet might bear the verses.

Ros. Ay, but the feet were lame, and could not bear themselves without the verse, and therefore stood lamely in the verse.

Cel. But didst thou hear, without wondering how thy name should be hang'd and carv'd upon these trees ?

Ros. ~~I was seven of the nine days out of the won~~der, before you came ; for look here what I found on a palm-tree : I was never so be-rhymed since Pythago-

~~ras' time, that I was an Irish rat, which I can hardly remember.~~

Cel. Trow you, who hath done this?

Ros. Is it a man?

Cel. And a chain, that you once wore, about his neck: Change you colour?

Ros. I pr'ythee, who?

Cel. O lord, lord! it is a hard matter for friends to meet; but mountains may be removed with earthquakes, and so encounter.

Ros. Nay, but who is it?

Cel. Is it possible?

Ros. Nay, I pray thee now, with most petitionary vehemence, tell me who it is.

Cel. O wonderful, wonderful, and most wonderful wonderful, and yet again wonderful, and after that out of all whooping!

Ros. Good my complexion! dost thou think, though I am caparison'd like a man, I have a doublet and hose in my disposition? ~~One inch of delay more is a South-sea off discovery.~~ I pr'ythee, tell me, who is it? quickly, and speak apace: ~~I would thou couldst stammer, that thou might'st pour~~ this concealed man out of thy mouth, as wine comes out of a narrow-mouth'd bottle; either too much at once, or none at all. I pr'ythee take the cork out of thy mouth, that I may drink thy tidings.

Cel. So you may put a ma~~n in your belly.~~

~~*Ros.* Is he of God's making?~~ What manner of man? Is his head worth a hat, or his chin worth a beard?

Cel. Nay, he hath but a little beard.

Ros. Why, ~~God~~ Heaven will send more, if the man will be

Sheep Bell heard occasionally thro' the Scene.

TWO ROSALINDS

The crucial role in the play was of course that of Rosalind, as acted by Louisa Nisbett, whom Macready had attached to his company during the summer especially to play the part. Mrs. Nisbett, at the age of thirty, rivalled Mme. Vestris for reputation as the finest comedienne of the day. A stunningly beautiful and intensely vivacious woman, she was much loved in such roles as Lady Teazle, Helen in Knowles's *The Hunchback*, Constance in Knowles's *The Love Chase*, and Lady Gay Spanker in Boucicault's *London Assurance*, which she had created at Covent Garden only the season before. The men of the green room adored her. One of them, Westland Marston, would describe her in after years as more genuinely beautiful and captivating than the Vestris: "Her forehead, though rather low, was wide, her eyes brilliant and expressive; the oval of her clear face was relieved and thrown out by a waving wreath of dark hair. Her neck was long and stately, her form lithe and elastic, and her stature tall. . . . Mrs. Nisbett had a laugh which swept away and charmed one by its freshness and fullness, by its music, and by its union of refinement with *abandon*" (*Our Recent Actors*, II, 151). Samuel Phelps, who played Adam, was forever remembering her voice, her laugh, her eyes, "her gorgeous neck and shoulders—her superbly symmetrical limbs—her grace, her taste, her nameless but irresistible charm"; and John Ryder, the Banished Duke, told John Coleman that he would have made himself a door-mat for her if he had had the chance (*Players and Playwrights*, I, 167, 307). When *Pendennis* appeared, in 1850, it was common green room gossip (probably mistaken) that Mrs. Nisbett was the original of the bovine Fotheringay: the actors denied the likeness furiously and savaged Thackeray for libelling her.

The critical reception of her Rosalind, however, was not unmitigated praise. The reviewer for the *Athenaeum*, for instance, allowed that "she becomes the doublet and hose well, and utters the mirthful pleasantries with such relish of the sport, that it is impossible not to enjoy the merriment she provokes"; but he began his account with the proposition that "Mrs. Nisbett, as may be supposed, does not sound the depths of the character." The *Times*, while allowing her "agreeable enough" and acknowledging the great applause she received, felt that she "did not certainly fulfill every requisite of the character. Joyous indeed she was and merry, but it was not the joy and merriment of the banished Duke's daughter; it betrayed no inward heaviness of heart, it was thoughtless when it should have been thoughtful: in short, there was an absence of that graceful sensibility which is the very soul of the character, and without which it loses all its poetry." *John Bull* thought her acceptable in the brilliant parts, but lacking in affection towards Celia in the first act. The *Literary Gazette* found her "rather too buoyant," perhaps too much a "rattle." The *Atlas*, perhaps carpingly, claimed to be grieved by "the evident want of study she betrays," and accused her of "errors of reading of the most apparent grossness."

The fact was that the character of Rosalind was just at this point passing through the final stage of metamorphosis from an eighteenth century hoyden, a comic breeches part, into the sentimental "womanly woman" so cherished throughout Victorian times. One might pinpoint the transition as occurring in this very season and production, though Macready himself was slow to become aware of it. His regular leading lady, Helen Faucit, was the perfect representative for the Rosalind of the new generation; when he passed her over and imported Mrs. Nisbett for the part he was in effect dreaming of Dora Jordan, living in the past. In the first week of December, 1842, Mrs. Nisbett was ill and Miss Faucit substituted for her (December 1 and 7; she also played Rosalind for the Queen's Command on June 12). The occasion meant so little to Macready that he neglected even to mention it in his diary; but there was a prophet standing by ready to acclaim Miss Faucit, and the occasion became the real beginning of the life of Rosalind as a Victorian gentlewoman.

The prophet's name was George Fletcher. His essays on Shakespeare, collected in 1847 under the title *Studies of Shakespeare*, were a significant expression of the times. He saw keenly what he wanted to see, and he wrote with a sharp pen. According to Sir Theodore Martin, Miss Faucit's husband and biographer, Fletcher "was a man of very recluse habits, but had yielded to the solicitation of friends to go and judge for himself of Miss Faucit as an interpreter of Shakespeare" (*Helena Faucit*, p. 93). He was so enlightened by her performances of Constance, Rosalind, Imogen, and the rest, that he felt obliged to write about them at length, and further, Sir Theodore tells us, "he owed much to what he learned from her conversation as well as from her acting." Macready knew Fletcher but slightly and could not endure him. In diarizing a dull dinner party in March, 1841, he described Fletcher as "a wretched 'dust'," and blamed himself very little for having been "very intolerant . . . in the conversation with that uninformed, assuming, talking 'dust'." The hostility thankful: let me stay the growth of his beard, if thou delay me not the knowledge of his chin.

Cel. It is young Orlando; that tripp'd up the wrestler's heels, and your heart, both in an instant.

Ros. Nay, but the devil take mocking; speak sad brow, and true maid.

Cel. I'faith, coz, 'tis he.

Ros. Orlando?

Cel. Orlando.

Ros. Alas the day! what shall I do with my doublet and hose?—What did he, when thou saw'st him? What said he? How look'd he? Wherein went he? What makes he here? Did he ask for me? Where remains he? How parted he with thee? and when shalt thou see him again? Answer me in one word.

Cel. You must borrow me Garagantua's mouth first: 'tis a word too great for any mouth of this age's size: To say, ay, and no, to these particulars, is more than to answer in a catechism.

Ros. But doth he know that I am in this forest, and in man's apparel? Looks he as freshly as he did the day he wrestled?

Cel. It is as easy to count atomies, as to resolve the propositions of a lover:—but take a taste of my finding him, and relish it with a good observance. I found him under a tree, like a dropp'd acorn.

Ros. It may well be call'd Jove's tree, when it drops forth such fruit.

Cel. Give me audience, good madam.

Ros. Proceed.

Cel. There lay he, stretch'd along, like a wounded knight.

Ros. ~~Though it be pity to see such a sight, it well~~
becomes the ground.

Cel. ~~Cry,~~ holla! to ~~thy tongue, I pr'ythee; it cur~~
~~vets very un easonably.~~ He was furnish'd like a hunter.

Ros. O ominous! he comes to kill my heart.

Cel. I would sing my song without a burden: thou
bring'st me out of tune.

Ros. Do you not know I am a woman? when I think
I must speak. Sweet, say on.

Enter ORLANDO *and* JAQUES.

Cel. You bring me out:—Soft! comes he not here?

Ros. 'Tis he; slink by, and note him.

[CELIA *and* ROSALIND *retire.*

Jaq. I thank you for your company; but, good faith,
I had as lief have been myself alone.

Orl. And so had I; but yet, for fashion sake, I thank
you too for your society.

Jaq. ~~God~~ Heaven be with you; let's meet as little as we can.

Orl. I do desire we may be better strangers.

Jaq. I pray you, mar no more trees with writing
love-songs in their barks.

Orl. I pray you, mar no more of my verses with
reading them ill-favouredly.

Jaq. Rosalind is your love's name?

Orl. Yes, just.

Jaq I do not like her name.

Orl. There was no thought of pleasing you, when
she was christen'd.

Jaq. What stature is she of?

Orl. Just as high as my heart.

was mutual. In the essays, while crying up the beauties of "our first living actress," Fletcher awards Macready only grudging praise. In the 1847 Preface, indeed, he refers to Macready as "the chief melodramatic actor of the day," regrets that he is still accepted as "a hero of Shakespearian tragedy," and congratulates Miss Faucit (now no longer associated with Macready) for having been set free from "the oppressive contact of an uncongenial style."

In his first essay, which appeared in the *Athenaeum* on February 4, 1843, he speaks of her December appearances in Rosalind, in which, he asserts, she managed "to infuse into the part . . . all the tender though lively grace which the poet has made its principal attribute and most exquisite attraction—breathing the soul of elegance, wit, and feeling, through that noble forest pastoral." The implication is obvious: what Miss Faucit did, Mrs. Nisbett did not do. In the summer of 1844, a year after the Macready management had ended, Fletcher published a series of four papers on *As You Like It* in which he spelled out his views of the case at length. Not only was Mrs. Nisbett wrong in her approach to Rosalind, but so too in her time was Mrs. Jordan and so too apparently were all other actresses until Miss Faucit created "the very Rosalind" of Shakespeare. The error goes back to the Restoration period, he argues, "when, under the ascendancy which the restored court gave to French principles of taste and criticism, it was sought to subject even the great *ideal dramas* of Shakespeare to the commonplace classical circumscriptions of *tragedy* and *comedy*." He does not pause to consider what the words "tragedy" and "comedy" might have meant to the Elizabethans; he is hot on the trace of current green room sins. "This great, unique, ideal play being once definitively set down upon the manager's books as a comedy in the limited sense, it followed of course, according to theatrical reasoning, that the part of its heroine was evermore to be sustained by whatever lady should be regarded, by distinction, as the *comic* actress for the time being." Only under this false principle could Mrs. Jordan have been assigned the role, for in spite of all her genuine comic powers everything about her—"the figure, the spirit, or the manner"— was for Fletcher shockingly unsuited to the "heavenly Rosalind." Macready stands convicted of wholly misunderstanding Shakespeare when he perpetuated "the old green room notion" and chose Mrs. Nisbett (Lady Gay Spanker) for Rosalind.

What is needed to restore the role from the vulgar popular conception of it, Fletcher says, is "a true Shakespearian actress, in the highest and most peculiar sense of the term. She must no more be either a tragic or a comic performer, in the limited and exclusive sense, than the 'As You Like It' is a comedy, or 'Cymbeline', for instance, is a tragedy, in the narrow signification." Such an actress is, of course, Helen Faucit—"of highest and truest Shakespearian genius that we possess." Unfortunately the London stage had now fallen into such lamentable condition that Miss Faucit's Rosalind could be seen only in the provinces. Fletcher excerpts a paragraph from *The Edinburgh Chronicle* to enhance his own opinion: "As we have but too often seen the Rosalind of the stage, she was merely the pretty coquette, roguish and know-ing in the small artifices of a cold nature; or, what is worse, a coarse and not over nice woman of fashion, who has laid down her maidenhood with her dress, as if she thought, in despite of the author, that it was actually necessary that she should wear doublet and hose in her disposition. How different is it with this lady's Rosalind! In the most joyous outbusts of her sparkling fancy amid the freedom of the forest, we never miss the duke's daughter, whom, in the first act, we have seen, in the gentleness and unconscious grace of her deportment, the leading ornament of the court of her usurping uncle. She is never less than the high-born and high-bred gentlewoman."

It was Miss Faucit's kind of Rosalind that prevailed during the long remainder of the century. The sentiments of John Coleman, who first supported her in the provinces as Sylvius and later grew up to Orlando, are typical of the rising generation: "It was reserved for *my* Rosalind to develop the poetic side of the character, and to present an

Ⓠ / turn from him. /

impersonation of surpassing subtlety and grace—of dignity and delicacy, of truth and beauty—an impersonation, interpenetrated (even amidst its most innocent and ingenuous ebulliences of delight) with pathetic minors and tremulous undertones of langorous passion—passion impermeated with love-breathing sighs, sunny smiles, and delicate tears, which always thrilled at least one auditor with a strange emotion" (*Players and Playwrights*, I, 170). Eventually even Macready came to realize that his casting of Mrs. Nisbett had been an "error". She was "the only shortcoming in the whole performance," he told Lady Pollock; "a very charming actress in many characters, but not equal to that. She was not disagreeable, but she was inadequate" (*Macready As I Knew Him*, p. 21).

Forty years later Helen Faucit published an essay on Rosalind (collected in *Some of Shakespeare's Female Characters*, 1885), in which, as to be expected, she repeats Fletcher's *caveat* against assigning "comic" actresses to the role. She suggests that this "strange perversion" of which "we read" could have happened only in the distant past. Her reflections on the character are unbearably sentimental. Though it may be unfair to judge her stage art by what she writes about it, yet the assurance, even the ecstasy, in which she dwells upon "the glad rapture of the tender passion," "the sweet little womanly question," "herself loving deeply, and prizing a good man's love as her best treasure," "her pretty womanly waywardness playing like summer lightning over her throbbing tenderness of heart," suggests that we could no more endure her Rosalind than the rowdiest hoyden who ever romped the part. Mrs. Nisbett's way, whatever its faults were, might tempt us more.

Jaq. You are full of pretty answers : Have you not been acquainted with goldsmiths' wives, and conn'd them out of rings?

~~*Orl.* No so ; but I answer you right painted cloth, from whence you have studied your questions.~~

Jaq. ~~You have a nimble wit ; I think it was made of Atalanta's heels.~~ Will you sit down with me? and we two will rail against our mistress the world, and all our misery.

Orl. I will chide no breather in the world, but myself ; against whom I know most faults.

Jaq. The worst fault you have, is to be in love.

Orl. 'Tis a fault I will not change for your best virtue.   I am weary of you.

Jaq. By my troth, I was seeking for a fool, when I found you.

Orl. He is drown'd in the brook ; look but in, and you shall see him.

Jaq. There I shall see mine own figure.

Orl. Which I take to be either a fool, or a cypher.

Jaq. I'll tarry no longer with you : farewell, good signior love.   *[Exit R.-]*

Orl. I am glad of your departure ; adieu, good monsieur melancholy.   *[Exit L.-]*

[~~Exit Jaques.~~—CELIA *and* ROSALIND *come forward.*   - R.-

Ros. I will speak to him like a saucy lacquey, and under that habit play the knave with him.—Do you hear, forester?

[with] *Orl.* Very well ; What would you?—/ *Re-enters L.-*/

Ros. I pray you, what is't o' clock?

Orl. You should ask me, what time o'day ; there's no clock in the forest.

Ros. Then there is no true lover in the forest; else sighing every minute, and groaning every hour, would detect the lazy foot of time, as well as a clock.

Orl. And why not the swift foot of time? had not that been as proper?

Ros. By no means, sir: Time travels in divers paces with divers persons: I'll tell you who time ambles withal, who time trots withal, who time gallops withal, and who he stands still withal.

Orl. I pr'ythee, who doth he trot withal?

Ros. Marry, he trots hard with a young maid, between the contract of her marriage, and the day it is solemnized: if the interim be but a se'nnight, time's pace is so hard, that it seems the length of seven years.

Orl. Who ambles time withal?

Ros. With a priest that lacks Latin, and a rich man that hath not the gout; for the one sleeps easily, because he cannot study; and the other lives merrily, because he feels no pain: ~~the one lacking the burden of lean and wasteful learning; the other knowing no burden of heavy tedious penury~~: These time ambles withal.

Orl. Who doth he gallop withal?

Ros. With a thief to the gallows: for though he go as softly as foot can fall, he thinks himself too soon there.

Orl. Who stays it still withal?

Ros. With lawyers in the vacation: for they sleep between term and term, and then they perceive not how time moves.

Orl. Where dwell you, pretty youth?

FANNY STIRLING'S CELIA

Mrs. Stirling was a great favorite in Celia, being frequently compared to Mrs. Nisbett to the latter's disadvantage. A fine comedienne of twenty-seven, she had been on the stage for just ten years. John Coleman records Samuel Phelps's memory of her as "a deuced fine woman in those days", and John Ryder's that she was "then as fine a woman as ever stepped in shoe-leather" (*Players and Playwrights*, I, 167, 307). *John Bull* declared her "the best representative of Celia we have seen." The *Spectator* thought her Celia "cordial in its sprightliness, and showing a deep sensibility under its graceful vivacity." The *Examiner* described her performing as "the prettiest, quietest, most sensible, most graceful, and, if we may say so, open-hearted piece of acting we have seen of that kind for many a day."

⊙ / bel' adit' R : /

⊘ / X'es with bel' to L : /

Ros. With this shepherdess, my sister; here in the
skirts of this forest, like fringe upon a petticoat. ☺   *6.-*

~~*Orl.* Are you native of this place?~~
Ros. As the coney, that you see dwell where she is
kindled.

Orl. Your accent is something finer than you could   *L.-*
purchase in so removed a dwelling.

Ros. I have been told so of many: but, indeed, an
old religious uncle of mine taught me to speak, who
was in his youth an in-land man; one that knew court-
ship too well, for there he fell in love. I have heard
him read many lectures against it; and I thank ~~God~~, I   ∧ *Heaven*
am not a woman, to be touch'd with so many giddy
offences as he hath generally tax'd their whole sex
withal.

Orl. Can you remember any of the principal evils,
that he laid to the charge of women?

Ros. There were none principal: they were all like
one another, as half-pence are; every one fault seeming monstrous, till his fellow fault came to match it.

Orl. I pr'ythee, recount some of them.

Ros. No; I will not cast away my physick, but on
those that are sick. There is a man haunts the forest,
that abuses our young plants with carving Rosalind on
their barks; hangs odes upon hawthorns, and elegies
on brambles; all, forsooth, deifying the name of Rosalind: if I could meet that fancy-monger, I would give
him some good counsel, for he seems to have the quo-
tidian of love upon him.

Orl. I am he that is so love-shaked; I pray you, tell
me your remedy.

Ros. There is none of my uncle's marks upon you:

he taught me how to know a man in love; in which cage of rushes, I am sure, you are not prisoner.

Orl. What were his marks?

Ros. A lean cheek; which you have not: a blue eye, and sunken; which you have not: an unquestionable spirit; which you have not: a beard neglected; which you have not :— but I pardon you for that; for, simply, your having in beard is a younger brother's revenue: Then your hose should be ungarter'd, your bonnet unbanded, your sleeve unbuttoned, your shoe untied, and every thing about you demonstrating a careless desolation. But you are no such man; you are rather point-device in your accoutrements; as loving yourself, than seeming the lover of any other.

Orl. Fair youth, I would I could make thee believe I love.

Ros. Me believe it? you may as soon make her that you love believe it; which, I warrant, she is apter to do, than to confess she does: that is one of the points in the which women still give the lie to their consciences. But, in good sooth, are you he that hangs the verses on the trees, wherein Rosalind is so admired?

Orl. I swear to thee, youth, by the white hand of Rosalind, I am that he, that unfortunate he.

Ros. But are you so much in love as your rhymes speak?

Orl. Neither rhyme nor reason can express how much.

Ros. Love is merely a madness; and, I tell you, deserves as well a dark house and a whip, as madmen do: and the reason why they are not so punished and cured,

4.

Touch-tone.

Audrey.

Jaques.

5.-

Zür Glaser Mundart.

is, that the lunacy is so ordinary, that the whippers are in love too: Yet I profess curing it by counsel.

Orl. Did you ever cure any so?

Ros. Yes, one; and in this manner.   He was to imagine me his love, his mistress; and I set him every day to woo me: At which time would I, being but a moonish youth, grieve, be effeminate, changeable, longing, and liking; proud, fantastical, apish, shallow, inconstant, full of tears, full of smiles; for every passion something, and for no passion truly any thing, as boys and women are for the most part cattle of this colour: would now like him, now loath him; then entertain him, then forswear him; now weep for him, then spit at him; that I drave my suitor from his mad humour of love, to a living humour of madness; ~~which was, to forswear the full stream of the world, and to live in a nook merely monastick~~: And thus I cured him; and this way will I take upon me to wash your liver as clean as a sound sheep's heart, that there shall not be one spot of love in't.

Orl. I would not be cured, youth.

Ros. I would cure you, if you would but call me Rosalind, and come every day to my cote, and woo me.

Orl. Now, by the faith of my love, I will; tell me where it is.

Ros. Go with me to it, and I'll show it you: and, by the way, you shall tell me where in the forest you live:—Will you go?

Orl. With all my heart, good youth.

Ros. Nay, you must call me Rosalind:—Come, sister, will you go?   [*Exeunt.*

~~SCENE III.~~

R-21 C.-

Enter TOUCHSTONE *and* AUDREY; JAQUES *at a distance, observing them.*

Touch. Come apace, good Audrey; I will fetch up your goats, Audrey: And how, Audrey? am I the man yet? Doth my simple feature content you?

Aud. Your features! Lord warrant us! what features?

Touch. I am here with thee and thy goats, as the most capricious poet, honest Ovid, was among the Goths.

Jaq. O knowledge ill-inhabited! worse than Jove in a thatch'd house!   */at back-* [*Aside.*]

Touch. When a man's verses cannot be understood, nor a man's good wit seconded with the forward child, understanding, it strikes a man more dead than a great reckoning in a little room:—Truly, I would the gods had made thee poetical.

Aud. I do not know what poetical is: Is it honest in deed and word? Is it a true thing?

Touch. No, truly; for the truest poetry is the most feigning; and lovers are given to poetry; and what they swear in poetry, may be said, as lovers, they do feign.

Aud. Do you wish then, that the gods had made me poetical?

Touch. I do, truly: for thou swear'st to me, thou art honest; now, if thou wert a poet, I might have some hope thou didst feign.

Aud. Would you not have me honest?

RESTORATION OF SIR OLIVER MARTEXT. In this passage (Folio, III. 3) Macready deprived Touchstone for the first time of his discourse on "horns" and of his rhyme line "we must live in bawdry," but his restoration of the scene as a whole is significant: Sir Oliver Martext had not appeared on the stage for over two centuries, nor had Jaques been present to comment on the scene and dissuade Touchstone from the false wedding.

No apple, - or turnip munching - mind, Audrey!

AUDREY'S APPLE. The stage-direction was apparently an oral one from Macready to the actress, which Ellis thought remarkable enough to write down. Audrey's preoccupation with apples and turnips is a long story, amusingly traced by Professor Sprague from 1825 to the end of the century (*Shakespeare and the Actors*, p. 37). The tradition is probably much older. Sprague does not mention Macready's abrogation of it.

*Rosalind
Celia.*

AUDREY : head dress blue over white; neckpiece white; dress tan trimmed with brown; sleeves gray; apron white; petticoat blue; stockings red; shoes black.

CLOWN (WILLIAM) : pencil sketch.

TOUCHSTONE : hat and pouch red; collar and sleeves green; jacket brown trimmed with black; legs gray.

Touch. No truly, unless thou wert hard-favour'd: for honesty coupled to beauty, is to have honey a sauce to sugar.

Jaq. A material fool!   [*Aside.*

Aud. Well, I am not fair; and therefore I pray the gods make me honest!

Touch. Truly, and to cast away honesty upon a foul slut, were to put good meat in an unclean dish.

Aud. I am not a slut, though I thank the gods I am foul.

Touch. Well, praised be the gods for thy foulness! sluttishness may come hereafter. But be it as it may be, I will marry thee: and to that end, I have been with Sir Oliver Mar-text, the vicar of the next village; who hath promised to meet me in this place of the forest, and to couple us.

Jaq. I would fain see this meeting.   [*Aside.*

Aud. Well, the gods give us joy!

Touch. Amen. A man may, if he were of a fearful heart, stagger in this attempt; for here we have no temple but the wood, no assembly but horn-beasts. But what though? Courage! As horns are odious, they are necessary. It is said,—Many a man knows no end of his goods: right: many a man has good horns, and knows no end of them. Well, that is the dowry of his wife; tis none of his own getting. Horns? Even so:——Poor men alone?——No, no; the noblest deer hath them as huge as the rascal. Is the single man therefore blessed? No: as a wall'd town is more worthier than a village, so is the forehead of a married man more honourable than the bare brow of a batchelor: and by how much defence is better than no skill, by so much is a horn more precious than to want.

Enter Sir OLIVER MAR-TEXT. *R-21 C.-*

Here comes sir Oliver :—Sir Oliver Mar-text, you are
well met : Will you despatch us here under this tree,
or shall we go with you to your chapel ?

/ *down, R* /   *Sir Oli.* Is there none here to give the woman ?

~~*Touch.* I will not take her on gift of any man.~~

Sir Oli. Truly, she must be given, or the marriage
is not lawful.

Jaq. [*Discovering himself.*] Proceed, proceed ; I'll
give her.

Touch. Good even, good master *What ye call't :* How
do you, sir ? You are very well met : ~~God~~'ild you for

∧ *Heaven*   your last company : I am very glad to see you :—Even
a toy in hand here, sir :—Nay, pray be cover'd.

Jaq. Will you be married, motley ?

Touch. As the ox hath his bow, sir, the horse his
curb, and the faulcon her bells, so man hath his desires ; and as pigeons bill, so wedlock would be nib-
bling.

Jaq. And will you, being a man of your breeding,
be married under a bush, like a beggar ? Get you to
church, and have a good priest that can tell you what
marriage is : this fellow will but join you together as
they join wainscoat ; then one of you will prove a
shrunk pannel, and, like green timber, warp, warp.

Touch. I am not in the mind but I were better to be
married of him than of another : for he is not like to
marry me well ; and not being well married, it will be
a good excuse for me hereafter to leave my wife.

[*Aside.*

Jaq. Go thou with me, and let me counsel thee.

5

∧ / act'g quickly, down L:- /

∧ / X'es to Jaques. /

7.-

⎡ Corin
⎢ Silvius
⎢ Phœbe
⎣ / Spoon Brook. /

◊ / X'g to R - looks earnestly at Touch'. /

THE STAGING OF III. 3 (Folio, III. 4 and 5) (201 lines cut to 128). A pair of flats came together in the second grooves depicting sky and forest, and a set piece was thrust on in the second entrance right to represent Rosalind's "lodge in the wilderness, overgrown with creeping plants." It is sunrise. "The songs of birds are heard all around, gently decreasing," Macready wrote in his own book. Ellis does not mention the birds, but Willmott has three cues for them, plus "Birds to finish" at the act end; the critic of the *Spectator* reported them. * * * At the junction of the two scenes that make up this one scene, Macready had to tinker a few words to avoid change of locale.

Touch. Come, sweet Audrey ; /✗ R.- /
We must be married, ~~or we must live in bawdry~~.
Farewell, good master Oliver !

/ *sings.* /- Not—O sweet Oliver,
            O brave Oliver,
        Leave me not behi' thee ;
            But—Wind away,
            Begone, I say,
        I will not to wedding wi' thee.
        [*Exeunt* JAQUES, TOUCHSTONE, *and* AUDREY, R.- /
    Sir Oli. 'Tis no matter; ne'er a fantastical knave of
them all shall flout me out of my calling. —— [*Exit,* R.-2l C.- /

    3rd
SCENE IV.—*The same.*   *Before a Cottage.* / Sunrise / 2 gr.
            /.-   2.-
        Enter ROSALIND *and* CELIA. R.-2 C.-

Ros. Never talk to me, I will weep.
Cel. Do, I pr'ythee; but yet have the grace to con-
sider, that tears do not become a man.
Ros. But have I not cause to weep?
Cel. As good cause as one would desire; therefore
weep.

~~Ros. His very hair is of the dissembling colour.~~
Cel. Something browner than Judas's : marry, his
kisses are Judas's own children.
Ros. I'faith, his hair is of a good colour.
Cel. An excellent colour: your chesnut was ever the
only colour.
Ros. And his kissing is as full of sanctity as the touch
of holy bread.

Cel. ~~He hath bought a pair of cast lips of Diana: a nun of winter's sisterhood kisses not more religiously; the very ice of chastity is in them.~~

Ros. ~~But~~ Why did he swear he would come this morning, and comes not?

Cel. Nay certainly, there is no truth in him.

Ros. Do you think so?

Cel. Yes: ~~I think he is not a pick-purse, nor a horse-stealer; but for his verity in love, I do think him as concave as a cover'd goblet, or a worm-eaten nut.~~

Ros. Not true in love?

Cel. Yes, when he is in; but, I think he is not in.

Ros. You have heard him swear downright, he was.

Cel. *Was* is not *is :* besides, the oath of a lover is no stronger than the word of a tapster; they are both the confirmers of false reckonings: He attends here in the forest on the duke your father.

Ros. I met the duke yesterday, and had much question with him: He asked me, of what parentage I was; I told him, of as good as he; so he laugh'd, and let me go. But what talk we of fathers, when there is such a man as Orlando?

Cel. O, that's a brave man! he writes brave verses, speaks brave words, swears brave oaths, and breaks them bravely, ~~quite traverse, athwart the heart of his lover; as a puny~~ tilter, that spurs his horse but on one side, breaks his staff like a noble goose: ~~but all's brave, that youth mounts, and folly guides~~:—Who comes here?

Enter CORIN.

Cor. Mistress, and master, you have oft enquired

1

THE KEELEYS: TOUCHSTONE AND AUDREY

The famous comedy team of Robert Keeley and his wife Mary Ann drew a great deal of comment upon their Touchstone and Audrey. Every since their marriage in 1829, managers had tended to bill them together in parts ranging from the pathetic to the low comic, and authors of the minor drama deliberately contrived roles for them. They were enormously popular. "Both created laughter in their own way . . . as when did they ever fail to do so?" said *The Times* critic (who, as a matter of fact, thought them both wrong on this occasion).

Robert Keeley as Touchstone would appear to have been a clear case of miscasting. He was diminutive, ugly, and forty-nine years old—so far so good. But he was a Will Kempe, not a Robert Armin; or, as Colley Cibber wrote of Cave Underhill, "his particular excellence was in characters that may be called still-life, I mean the stiff, the heavy, and the stupid." His effective Shakespearean roles were of the order of Dogberry, Verges, and the Capulets' Peter. Westland Marston has memorialized him vividly in *Our Recent Actors* (II, 99): "In the display of a mind staggered by responsibilities and dangers to which it was ludicrously unequal; or, on rare occasions, evincing desperate temerity like that of a stag at bay; or possessed by a stupid, satisfied immobility, when instant action was needed; or by the infirmities of age, vacant and yielding, but with enough perception to give a fatuous gleam of intelligence—in all these Keeley was unrivalled in his day." This sounds at once delightful and extremely unlike Touchstone, and so almost unanimously the critics reported him. He "wanted the pompous fluency and oracular pedantry which are essential to the character," said *The Times*. The *Illustrated London News* found him "vigorously droll" but not "artist" enough to deliver a true Touchstone: he "had all the sheepishness, but the lighting up of the occasional soul—the flash and glow of the inner man—was a too visible deficiency under the dull exterior." The *Literary Gazette* complained of "an occasional stolidity" where there ought to have been "shrewdness of observation and caustic bitingness of speech." Only *John Bull*, while noticing the same deficiency of "intellectual quickness" that everyone objected to, managed to warp it around to a compliment: in departing from stage tradition Keeley was essaying "an approach to the true idea." But *John Bull*'s main point of approval was on "moral" rather than esthetic grounds. He was delighted to see the role cast to an actor of such small stature and physical unattractiveness: for had the "tall, good-looking, and over-conscious Clown of the Theatre" (Mat Howell?) played the part he could not have made "his presence with two beautiful ladies in a lonely wood, free from imputation!"

Mrs. Keeley, who indeed was held to be the more skilful actor of the two, came off rather better than her husband. She "was as full of mischief as an egg is full of meat," said John Ryder; "by Jove! she could act any mortal thing!" The *Literary Gazette* thought her Audrey was inimitable: "The lack-lustre inquisitive ignorance of her great lustrous eyes was superb: her thanking the gods for her foulness irresistibly laughable. We have seen other Audreys; we have seen Mrs. Gibbs, and there is a difference, yet we cannot but say that Mrs. Keeley entertained us as highly as we were ever entertained before." To the *Examiner* she was as "natural, rough, untutored, and unpoetical, as a member of the artless maiden's goat-flock might have been." Only *The Times* took notable exception to her as "hardly wild enough in her rusticity" and showing too much intelligence in her eye for "the dark, uncouth mind of the forest wench." No one particularly noticed her omission of Audrey's traditional business of mastication. Macready had flatly suppressed it (see page 62): "No apple—or turnip munching—mind, Audrey!"

Let us behold a

After the shepherd, that complain'd of love;
Who you saw sitting by me on the turf,
Praising the proud disdainful shepherdess,
That was his mistress.

    Cel. Well, and what of him?

    Cor. If you will see a pageant truly play'd,
Between the pale complexion of true love
And the red glow of scorn and proud disdain,
~~Go hence~~ a little, and I shall ~~conduct~~ you, *Retire*
If you will mark it.   *shew it*

    Ros. O come, let us remove;
The sight of lovers feedeth those in love:—
~~Bring us unto~~ this sight, and you shall say
I'll prove a busy actor in their play.   [~~Exeunt.~~

                      /All go up./

~~SCENE V.   Another Part of the Forest.~~
                2.-   *1.-*
       Enter SILVIUS *and* PHEBE.   *L.-*

    Sil. Sweet Phebe, do not scorn me; do not, Phebe:
Say, that you love me not; but say not so
In bitterness: The common executioner,
Whose heart the accustom'd sight of death makes hard,
Falls not the axe upon the humbled neck,
But first begs pardon: Will you sterner be
Than he that dies and lives by bloody drops?

~~Enter ROSALIND, CELIA, and CORIN, at a distance.~~

    Phe. I would not be thy executioner;
I fly thee, for I would not injure thee.
Thou tell'st me, there is murder in mine eye:
~~'Tis pretty, sure, and very probable,~~

That eyes,—that are the frail'st and softest things,
Who shut their coward gates on atomies,—
Should be call'd tyrants, butchers, murderers!
Now I do frown on thee with all my heart;
And, if mine eyes can wound, now let them kill thee;
Now counterfeit to swoon; why now fall down;
Or, if thou canst not, O, for shame, for shame,
Lie not, to say mine eyes are murderers.
Now show the wound mine eye hath made in thee:
Scratch thee but with a pin, and there remains
Some scar of it; lean but upon a rush,
The cicatrice and capable impressure
Thy palm some moment keeps: but now mine eyes,
Which I have darted at thee, hurt thee not;
Nor, I am sure, there is no force in eyes
That can do hurt.

   Sil. O dear Phebe,
If ever, (as that ever may be near,)
You meet in some fresh cheek the power of fancy,
Then shall you know the wounds invisible
That love's keen arrows make.

   Phe. But, till that time,
Come not thou near me : and, when that time comes,
Afflict me with thy mocks, pity me not;
As, till that time, I shall not pity thee. *R-*

   Ros. And why, I pray you? [*Advancing.*] Who might
        be your mother,   Λ
That you insult, exult, and all at once,
Over the wretched? What though you have more
        beauty,
(As, by my faith, I see no more in you
Than without candle may go dark to bed,)

PASTORAL PARODY. Macready economized nearly sixty lines on Silvius and Phebe (and incidentally on Rosalind), slashing down their scene pretty much according to stage tradition. Shakespeare's delicate parody of pastoralism and euphuism was probably not very meaningful to a generation not yet quite free from the elegant verbal roundabouts of the Pope-to-Wordsworth manners in "poetry." The sorriest cut is Phebe's lovely description of Rosalind-Ganymede (page 71); at first Macready inked out only a few lines of it, but finally he followed tradition and discarded it all.

PHEBE : hat and overdress white trimmed with red, yellow and blue flowers and green leaves; underdress pale yellow; blue ribbons on staff.

Must you be therefore proud and pitiless?
Why, what means this? Why do you look on me?
I see no more in you, than in the ordinary
Of nature's sale-work:—Od's my little life!
I think, she means to tangle my eyes too:—
No, 'faith, proud mistress, hope not after it; / ✗ C.-/
'Tis not your inky brows, your black-silk hair,
Your bugle eye-balls, nor your cheek of cream,
That can entame my spirits to your worship.
You foolish shepherd, wherefore do you follow her,
Like foggy south, puffing with wind and rain?
You are a thousand times a properer man,
Than she a woman: 'Tis such fools as you,
That make the world full of ill-favour'd children:
'Tis not her glass, but you, that flatters her;
And out of you she sees herself more proper,
Than any of her lineaments can show her.—
But, mistress, know yourself; down on your knees,
And thank heaven, fasting, for a good man's love:
For I must tell you friendly in your ear,—
Sell when you can; you are not for all markets:
Cry the man mercy; love him; take his offer;
Foul is most foul, being foul to be a scoffer.
So, take her to thee, shepherd;—fare you well. -/ ✗ L.-/ -/ ✗ C.-/
    Phe. Sweet youth, I pray you chide a year together;
I had rather hear you chide, than this man woo.
    Ros. He's fallen in love with her foulness, and she'll
fall in love with my anger: if it be so, as fast as she
answers thee with frowning looks, I'll sauce her with
bitter words.—Why look you so upon me?
    Phe. For no ill will I bear you.
    Ros. I pray you, do not fall in love with me,

For I am falser than vows made in wine:
Besides, I like you not: ~~If you will know my house,~~
~~'Tis at the tuft of olives, here hard by~~:—

Come,

Will you go, sister?—Shepherd, ply her hard:—
Come, sister.—Shepherdess, look on him better,
And be not proud: though all the world could see,
None could be so abus'd in sight as he.
Come, to our flock.

          [*Exeunt* ROSALIND, CELIA, *and* CORIN.

~~*Phe.* Dear shepherd! now I find thy saw of might;~~
~~*Who ever lov'd, that lov'd not at first sight?*~~

   Sil. Sweet Phebe,—
   Phe. Ha! what say'st thou, Silvius?
   Sil. Sweet Phebe, pity me.
   Phe. Why, I am sorry for thee, gentle Silvius.
   Sil. Wherever sorrow is, relief would be;
~~If you do sorrow at my grief in love,~~
By giving love, your sorrow and my grief
Were both extermin'd.
   Phe. Thou hast my love; Is not that neighbourly?
   ~~*Sil.* I would have you.~~
   Phe. ~~Why, that were covetousness.~~
Silvius, the time was, that I hated thee;
And yet it is not, that I bear thee love:
But since that thou canst talk of love so well,
Thy company, which erst was irksome to me,
I will endure; and I'll employ thee too:
But do not look for further recompense,
Than thine own gladness that thou art employ'd.
   ~~*Sil.* So holy, and so perfect is my love,~~
And I in such a poverty of grace,
That I shall think it a most plenteous crop,

⊘ / to bel.' – who X'es beh^d to X. – /

⊘ / still looking off after Ros.' – X. – /

⊘ / she appears delighted . /

THE LESSER ROLES

In recalling the production for Lady Pollock, Macready claimed that every part was well fitted, instancing the fact that he had persuaded James Hudson to play Le Beau. "Handsome Hudson," as he was known in the green room, was a big, good looking Irish comedian who had come to Macready from Dublin only the year before. When he entered Macready's office intending to decline the part, Macready forebade him to speak until the part was read to him. "Before the reading was concluded, Hudson was in convulsions of laughter, and delighted to take the character," assuring Macready that he "had no idea that it was" (*Macready As I Knew Him*, p. 21). Nearly every critic praised his bustling absurdity in the part or noticed the amount of applause and laughter he created. * * * John Ryder, then a newcomer to London, was chided for his provincial coarseness in the role of the Banished Duke, but was equally seen to promise well for the future. * * * Duke Frederick was said by one critic to have been "libelled" by George Bennett. Bennett was "superfluously brutal and coarse," said another—"one of the most conspicuous of those macadamizers of dialogue who break sentences into bits with the hammer of their emphasis." * * * Samuel Phelps's Adam was called "worthy," "an excellent and true piece of vivid and honest nature," "almost as good a representative as the late Mr. Murray, who was perfection in the part." * * * Henry Compton delivered William "in one most humorous gape of rustic astonishment," "rejected all the old artifices that provoked laughter," "was chaste and subdued, and did what was needed and no more." * * * Among the musical personnel, Allen was unanimously praised for his sweet singing of Amiens, Priscilla Horton for her rendering of the First Page, and Phillips, Stretton, Sims Reeves, and Miss Gould for their vocal support.

To glean the broken ears after the man
That the main harvest reaps: loose now and then
A scatter'd smile, and that I'll live upon.

　　Phe. Know'st thou the youth, that spoke to me ere
　　　　while?
　　Sil. Not very well, but I have met him oft;
And he hath bought the cottage, and the bounds,
That the old carlot once was master of.

^ this

　　Phe. Think not I love him, though I ask for him;
'Tis but a peevish boy:—yet he talks well:—
But what care I for words? yet words do well,
When he that speaks them pleases those that hear.
It is a pretty youth:—not very pretty:—
But, sure, he's proud; and yet his pride becomes him:
He'll make a proper man: The best thing in him
Is his complexion; and faster than his tongue
Did make offence, his eye did heal it up.
He is not tall; yet for his years he's tall:
His leg is but so so; and yet 'tis well:
There was a pretty redness in his lip;
A little riper and more lusty red
Than that mix'd in his cheek; 'twas just the difference
Betwixt the constant red, and mingled damask.
There be some women, Silvius, had they mark'd him
In parcels as I did, would have gone near
To fall in love with him: but, for my part,
I love him not, nor hate him not; and yet
I have more cause to hate him than to love him:
For what had he to do to chide at me?
He said, mine eyes were black, and my hair black;
And, now I am remember'd, scorn'd at me:
I marvel, why I answer'd not again:

~~But that's all one; omittance is no quittance.~~
I'll write to him a very taunting letter,
And thou shalt bear it; Wilt thou, Silvius?
    Sil. Phebe, with all my heart.
    Phe. I'll write it straight;
The matter's in my head, and in my heart:
I will be bitter with him, and passing short:
Go with me, Silvius.   [*Exeunt.*

THE PLAYING TIME OF ACT III. This act is the longest of all (784 lines cut to 604), but it played off faster than either of the preceding acts, at nearly twenty lines per minute. Ellis calls the act thirty minutes, and Willmott, in substantial agreement, jotted down "5 past 9". There are no songs in the act and only two slidings of scenery; and the stage is dominated by Rosalind in her gayest and swiftest manner.

Horns ready. — *R-U E.*
THE STAGING OF IV. 1 (Folio, IV. 1 and 2) (242 lines cut to 196). The act drop rose on the same scene—the cottage in the second entrance right and the forest flats in the second grooves.

The Horns of the Hunter, heard winding in the distance, as the Act Drop rises.

1.-

Rosalind.

Celia. /2ᵈ/

Jaques.

Orlando.

RESTORATION. Macready restored the Jaques-Rosalind dialogue which opens the act.

ACT IV.

SCENE I.—*The same.* / *The cottage - as before.* / Ⓠ

Enter ROSALIND, CELIA, *and* JAQUES. / *L:* /

Jaq. I pr'ythee, pretty youth, let me be better acquainted with thee.

Ros. They say, you are a melancholy fellow.

Jaq. I am so; I do love it better than laughing.

Ros. Those, that are in extremity of either, are abominable fellows; and betray themselves to every modern censure, worse than drunkards.

Jaq. Why, 'tis good to be sad and say nothing.

Ros. Why then, 'tis good to be a post.

Jaq. I have neither the scholar's melancholy, which is emulation; nor the musician's, which is fantastical; nor the courtier's, which is proud; nor the soldier's, which is ambitious; nor the lawyer's, which is politick; nor the lady's, which is nice; nor the lover's, which is all these: but it is a melancholy of mine own, compounded of many simples, extracted from many objects: and, indeed, the sundry contemplation of my travels, in which my often rumination wraps me, a most humorous sadness.

Ros. A traveller! By my faith, you have great reason to be sad: I fear, you have sold your own lands, to

see other men's; then, to have seen much, and to have
nothing, is to have rich eyes and poor hands.

Jaq. Yes, I have gained my experience.

Enter ORLANDO. *L.*

Ros. And your experience makes you sad: I had
rather have a fool to make me merry, than experience
to make me sad; and to travel for it too. **O**

Orl. Good day, and happiness, dear Rosalind!

Jaq. Nay then, ~~God~~ be wi' you, an you talk in blank
verse. /*X 'es hastily to R — and* ————→ [*Exit's.*/

^heaven in

Ros. Farewell, monsieur traveller: ~~Look, you lisp,
and wear strange suits; disable all the~~ benefits of your
own country; be out of love with your nativity, and almost chide God for making you that countenance you
~~are; or I will scarce think you have swam in a gondo-
la.~~—Why, how now, Orlando! where have you been
all this while? You a lover?—An you serve me such
another trick, never come in my sight more.

Orl. My fair Rosalind, I come within an hour of my
promise.

Ros. Break an hour's promise in love? He that will
divide a minute into a thousand parts, and break but a
part of the thousandth part of a minute in the affairs of
love, it may be said of him, that Cupid hath clap'd him
o'the shoulder, but I warrant him heart-whole.

Orl. Pardon me, dear Rosalind.

Ros. Nay, an you be so tardy, come no more in my
sight; I had as lief be woo'd of a snail. /*X L.*/

Orl. Of a snail?

Ros. Ay, of a snail; for though he comes slowly, he
carries his house on his head; a better jointure, I think,

Ø /Celia nods to Orl,- salutingly - and goes off R-2 E:/

CUTTINGS FOR MRS. GRUNDY. We have noticed earlier passages in which Macready cut the text for decorum's sake, sometimes according to tradition, sometimes by his own lights. But in this scene he expurgated Rosalind's love prate in a perfect rage of false delicacy. On page 75, though it was customary to suppress the quibble about "horns," no one had ever been so nice as to deny Rosalind her "Come, woo me, woo me." Next he struck out the "Very good orators" line, apparently in order to get rid of the vulgar word "spit" (and a later producer, presumably Vezin, absurdly restored it as "cough"). The next cut, which was traditional, manages to avoid the word "mistress." The cut on page 77, also traditional, deprives Rosalind of her pretty vow, "I do take thee, Orlando, for my husband." Celia's proposal on page 79 to "show the world what the bird hath done to her own nest" had to go, of course, following old custom. At the end of the scene (bottom of page 79) Macready made a very important restoration of the girls' exit and of Rosalind's playful lines about Cupid. He balked, however, at the phrase "bastard of Venus." In his own copy he wrote "boy of Venus," which finally became "child of Venus." At this point even Thomas Bowdler had unblinkingly printed "bastard."

than you can make a woman: ~~Besides, he brings his destiny with him.~~

Orl. What's that?

Ros. Why, horns; which such as you are fain to be beholden to your wives for; but he comes armed in his fortune, and prevents the slander of his wife.

Orl. Virtue is no horn-maker; and my Rosalind is virtuous.

Ros. And I am your Rosalind.

Cel. It pleases him to call you so; but he hath a Rosalind of a better leer than you.

Ros. Come, woo me, woo me; for now I am in a holiday humour, and like enough to consent.—What would you say to me now, an I were your very very Rosalind?

Orl. I would kiss, before I spoke.

Ros. Nay, you were better speak first; and when you were gravelled for lack of matter, you might take occasion to kiss. ~~Very good orators, when they are out, they will spit; and for lovers, lacking (God warn us!) matter, the cleanliest shift is to kiss.~~

Orl. How if the kiss be denied?

Ros. Then she puts you to entreaty, and there begins new matter.

~~*Orl.* Who could be out, being before his beloved mistress?~~

Ros. Marry, that should you, if I were your mistress; or I should think my honesty ranker than my wit.

Orl. What, of my suit?

Ros. ~~Not out of your apparel, and yet out of your suit.~~ Am not I your Rosalind?

4

Orl. I take some joy to say you are, because I would be talking of her.

Ros. Well, in her person, I say—I will not have you.

Orl. Then, in mine own person, I die.

Ros. No, faith, die by attorney. The poor world is almost six thousand years old, and in all this time there was not any man died in his own person, *videlicet*, in a love-cause. ~~Troilus had his brains dashed out with a Grecian club;~~ yet he did what he could to die before; and he is one of the patterns of love. Leander, he would have lived many a fair year, though Hero had turned nun, if it had not been for a hot midsummernight: for, good youth, he went but forth to wash him in the Hellespont, and, being taken with the cramp, was drowned; and the foolish chroniclers of that age ~~found it was Hero of Sestos. But these are all lies;~~ men have died from time to time, and worms have eaten them, but not for love.

Orl. I would not have my right Rosalind of this mind; for, I protest, her frown might kill me.

Ros. By this hand, it will not kill a fly: But come, now I will be your Rosalind in a more coming-on disposition; and ask me what you will, I will grant it.

Orl. Then love me, Rosalind.

Ros. Yes, faith will I, Fridays, and Saturdays, and all.

Orl. And wilt thou haue me?

Ros. Ay, and twenty such.

Orl. What say'st thou?

Ros. Are you not good?

Orl. I hope so.

2

Hors ready again. - R-H.B.-

2.

Jaques.

Amiens.

2nd & 3rd For.t Lords.

All the other Do.

All the Hunters

All the Attendants.

/ Dogs: - Deer on pole: - &c /

⊖ / Runs to cottage, and calls, - "Celia! - Sister! - Sister!" - Celia re-enters R-2 E, - Ros' puts her a' X to E, - /

Ros. Why then, can one desire too much of a good thing? Come, sister, you shall be the priest, and marry us.—Give me your hand, Orlando:—What do you say, sister?

Orl. Pray thee, marry us.

Cel. I cannot say the words.

Ros. You must begin,——*Will you, Orlando,*—

Cel. Go to:——Will you, Orlando, have to wife this Rosalind?

Orl. I will.

Ros. Ay, but when?

Orl. Why now; as fast as she can marry us.

Ros. Then you must say,—*I take thee, Rosalind, for wife.*

Orl. I take thee, Rosalind, for wife.

Ros. I might ask you for your commission; but,—I do take thee, Orlando, for my husband: There a girl goes before the priest; and, certainly, a woman's thought runs before her actions.

Orl. So do all thoughts; they are winged.

Ros. Now tell me, how long you would have her, after you have possessed her.

Orl. For ever, and a day.

Ros. Say a day, without the ever: No, no, Orlando; men are April when they woo, December when they wed: maids are May when they are maids, but the sky changes when they are wives. I will be more jealous of thee than a Barbary cock-pigeon over his hen; more clamorous than a parrot against rain; more new-fangled than an ape; more giddy in my desires than a monkey: I will weep for nothing, like Diana in the fountain, and I will do that when you are disposed to be merry: I will laugh like a hyen, and that when thou art inclined to sleep.

Orl. But will my Rosalind do so?

Ros. By my life, she will do as I do.

Orl. O, but she is wise.

Ros. Or else she could not have the wit to do this: the wiser, the waywarder: Make the doors upon a woman's wit, and it will out at the casement; shut that, and 'twill out at the key-hole; stop that, 'twill fly with the smoke out at the chimney.

Orl. A man that had a wife with such a wit, he might say,—*Wit, whither wilt?*

Ros. Nay, you might keep that check for it, till you met your wife's wit going to your neighbour's bed. *house*

Orl. And what wit could wit have, to excuse that?

Ros. Marry, to say,—she came to seek you there. You shall never take her without her answer, unless you take her without her tongue. O, that woman that cannot make her fault her husband's occasion, let her never nurse her child herself, for she will breed it like a fool.

Orl. For these two hours, Rosalind, I will leave thee. /× L·/

Ros. Alas, dear love, I cannot lack thee two hours.

Orl. I must attend the duke at dinner; by two o'clock I will be with thee again.

Ros. Ay, go your ways, go your ways;—I knew what you would prove; my friends told me as much, and I thought no less:—that flattering tongue of yours won me:—'tis but one cast away, and so,—come, death.—Two o'clock is your hour?

Orl. Ay, sweet Rosalind.

TAKING OUT AN IMPROVEMENT. For a hundred years it had been the custom to introduce here (at the end of the passage which Macready cut on page 78) the cuckoldry song "When daisies pied" from the end of *Love's Labor's Lost*. In 1741 Kitty Clive sang it as Celia; Mrs. Jordan was famous later for singing it as Rosalind. During the nineteenth century it was regularly grafted onto the "heavenly Rosalind," and by the 1840's both moral and literary purists were incensed by this "barbarism." Macready suppressed it, and was much praised for doing so. Professor Odell was quite wrong, incidentally, in asserting that Macready retained the song (*Shakespeare from Betterton to Irving*, II, 206). No one objected that Macready also suppressed the bonafide lines about "your wife's wit going to your neighbor's bed" which had magnetized the song into this scene in the first place.

♯♯ Horns - forte.

in

Ros. By my troth, and in good earnest, and so ~~God~~ *Heaven* mend me, and by all pretty oaths that are not dangerous, if you break one jot of your promise, or come one minute behind your hour, I will think you the most pathetical break-promise, and the most hollow lover, and the most unworthy of her you call Rosalind, that may be chosen out of the gross band of the unfaithful : therefore beware my censure, and keep your promise.

Orl. With no less religion, than if thou wert indeed my Rosalind : So, adieu.

Ros. Well, time is the old justice that examines all such offenders, and let time try : Adieu !

[*Exit* ORLANDO. *L.-*/

Cel. You have simply misus'd our sex in your love-prate : ~~we must have your doublet and hose plucked over your head, and shew the world what the bird hath done to her own nest.~~

Ros. O coz, coz, coz, my pretty little coz, that thou didst know how many fathom deep I am in love ! But it cannot be sounded ; my affection hath an unknown bottom, like the bay of Portugal.

Cel. Or rather, bottomless ; that as fast as you pour affection in, it runs out.

child

Ros. No, that same wicked ~~bastard~~ of Venus, that was begot of thought, conceived of spleen, and born of madness ; that blind rascally boy, that abuses every one's eyes, because his own are out, let him be judge how deep I am in love. I'll tell thee, Aliena, I cannot be out of the sight of Orlando : I'll go find a shadow, and sigh till he come.

Cel. And I'll sleep.

[*Exeunt, L-2 E.-*/

~~SCENE II.   *Another part of the Forest.*~~

Amiens, - 2ⁿᵈ & 3 Forest Lords, and 20 other Forest

Enter JAQUES *and* Lords, *in the habit of Foresters.* R - ⊘

Jaq. Which is he that killed the deer?

3ᵈ Lord. Sir, it was I.

Jaq. Let's present him to the duke, like a Roman conqueror; and it would do well to set the deer's horns upon his head, for a branch of victory:—Have you no song, forester, for this purpose?

2 Lord. Yes, sir.

Jaq. Sing it; 'tis no matter how it be in tune, so it make noise enough. /✗ to L corner /

(*Glee and* ~~SONG.~~ *Chorus.*)

  1. *What shall he have, that kill'd the deer?*
  2. *His leather skin, and horns to wear.*
       1. *Then sing him home:*
  Take thou no scorn, to wear the horn;   } The rest shall
  It was a crest ere thou wast born.   } bear this bur-
       1. *Thy father's father wore it:*   } den.
       2. *And thy father bore it:*
All. The horn, the horn, the lusty horn,
      Is not a thing to laugh to scorn.   [Exeunt.

SCENE III.—*The Forest.*

Enter ROSALIND *and* CELIA.

Ros. How say you now? Is it not past two o'clock? and here much Orlando!

RESTORATION. This scene (Folio, IV. 2) and song had not been staged, except in *Love in a Forest*, since Shakespeare's time. From the beginning of the act the hunters' horns had been heard from the distance, coming nearer. Now there emerged upon the stage Jaques and, except for the Duke, the whole personnel of Forest Lords and Hunters, with their weapons, dogs, and slain deer hung on a pole.

Q / carrying their game, - / a large Deer / with bows - spears - &c

3.—

Rosalind.

Celia.

Silvius

‡ H^n Letter, N° 3.—

Oliver

Blooded napkin

W.—

A Sheep-fold, on the banks of a stream, in the distance

THE STAGING OF IV. 2 (Folio, IV. 3) (183 lines cut to 169). The cottage and its flats drew off to reveal another forest scene, set in the third grooves, showing in the stage left half and at some distance a sheepfold on a hillside above the banks of a stream. Macready had written in his own book "A Sheep-fold near. Sheep-bells heard," but Marshall's painted "distance" prevailed and the bells were not heard here.

Cel. I warrant you, with pure love, and troubled
brain, he has ta'en his bow and arrows, and is gone
forth—to sleep: Look, who comes here.

Enter SILVIUS. *L.*

Sil. My errand is to you, fair youth;—
My gentle Phebe bid me give you this:
/X'g to Rosalind, ——*and* [*Giving a letter.*]
I know not the contents; but, as I guess,
By the stern brow, and waspish action
Which she did use as she was writing of it,
It bears an angry tenour: pardon me,
I am but as a guiltless messenger.

Ros. Patience herself would startle at this letter,
And play the swaggerer; bear this, bear all:
She says, I am not fair; that I lack manners;
She calls me proud; and, that she could not love me
Were men as rare as Phœnix; Od's my will!
Her love is not the hare that I do hunt:
Why writes she so to me?—Well, shepherd, well,
This is a letter of your own device.

Sil. No, I protest, I know not the contents;   *- C. -*
Phebe did write it.

Ros. Come, come, you are a fool,
And turn'd into the extremity of love.
A saw her hand: she has a leathern hand,
A freestone-colour'd hand; I verily did think
That her old gloves were on, but 'twas her hands;
She has a huswife's hand: but that's no matter:
I say, she never did invent this letter;
This is a man's invention, and his hand.

Sil. Sure, it is hers.

Ros. Why, 'tis a boisterous and cruel style,
A style for challengers; why, she defies me,
Like Turk to Christian : woman's gentle brain
Could not drop forth such giant-rude invention,
Such Ethiop words, blacker in their effect
Than in their countenance :—Will you hear the letter?
   Sil. So please you, for I never heard it yet;
Yet heard too much of Phebe's cruelty.
   Ros. She Phebes me : Mark how the tyrant writes.

> *Art thou god to shepherd turn'd,*   [Reads.
> *That a maiden's heart hath burn'd ?—*

Can a woman rail thus?
   Sil. Call you this railing?

   Ros. *Why, thy godhead laid apart,*
> *Warr'st thou with a woman's heart ?*

Did you ever hear such railing?—

> *Whiles the eye of man did woo me,*
> *That could do no vengeance to me.—*

Meaning me a beast.—

> *If the scorn of your bright eyne*
> *Have power to raise such love in mine,*
> *Alack, in me what strange effect*
> *Would they work in mild aspéct ?*
> *Whiles you chid me, I did love ;*
> *How then might your prayers move ?*

∧ /pointing off L:/

He, that brings this love to thee,
Little knows this love in me :
And by him seal up thy mind ;
Whether that thy youth and kind
Will the faithful offer take
Of me, and all that I can make ;
Or else by him my love deny,
And then I'll study how to die.

Sil. Call you this chiding?

Cel. Alas, poor shepherd !

Ros. Do you pity him? no, he deserves no pity.—
Wilt thou love such a woman?—What, to make thee
an instrument, and play false strains upon thee ! not to
be endured !—Well, go your way to her, (for I see,
love hath made thee a tame snake,) and say this to
her;—That if she love me, I charge her to love thee : if
she will not, I will never have her, unless thou entreat
for her.—If you be a true lover, hence, and not a word ;
for here comes more company.   [*Exit* SILVIUS.

Enter OLIVER,

Oli. Good-morrow, fair ones : Pray you, if you know
Where, in the purlieus of this forest, stands
A sheep-cote, fenc'd about with olive-trees ?

Cel. West of this place, down in the neighbour bot-
                tom,
The rank of osiers, by the murmuring stream,
Left on your right hand, brings you to the place :
But at this hour the house doth keep itself,
There's none within.

Oli. If that an eye may profit by a tongue,

Then I should know you by description;
Such garments, and such years: *The boy is fair,*
Of female favour, and bestows himself
Like a ripe sister: but the woman low,
And browner than her brother. Are not you
The owner of the house I did inquire for?

    Cel. It is no boast, being ask'd, to say, we are.

    Oli. Orlando doth commend him to you both;
And to that youth, he calls his Rosalind,
He sends this bloody napkin; Are you he?

    Ros. I am: What must we understand by this?

    Oli. Some of my shame; if you will know of me
What man I am, and how, and why, and where
This handkerchief was stain'd.

    Cel. I pray you, tell it.

    Oli. When last the young Orlando parted from you,
He left a promise to return again
Within an hour; and, pacing through the forest,
Chewing the food of sweet and bitter fancy,
Lo, what befel! he threw his eye aside,
And, mark, what object did present itself!
Under an oak, whose boughs were moss'd with age,
And high top bald with dry antiquity,
A wretched ragged man, o'ergrown with hair,
Lay sleeping on his back: about his neck
A green and gilded snake had wreath'd itself,
Who with her head, nimble in threats, approach'd
The opening of his mouth; but suddenly
Seeing Orlando, it unlink'd itself,
And with indented glides did slip away
Into a bush: under which bush's shade
A lioness, with udders all drawn dry,

Act II

Lay couching, head on ground, with catlike watch,
When that the sleeping man should stir; for 'tis
The royal disposition of that beast,
To prey on nothing that doth seem as dead:
This seen, Orlando did approach the man,
And found it was his brother, his elder brother.

    Cel. O, I have heard him speak of that same bro-
        ther;
And he did render him the most unnatural
That liv'd 'mongst men.

    Oli. And well he might so do,
For well I know he was unnatural.

    Ros. But, to Orlando;—Did he leave him there,
Food to the suck'd and hungry lioness?

    Oli. Twice did he turn his back, and purpos'd so:
But kindness, nobler ever than revenge,
And nature, stronger than his just occasion,
Made him give battle to the lioness,
Who quickly fell before him; in which hurtling
From miserable slumber I awak'd.

    Cel. Are you his brother?

    Ros. Was it you he rescu'd?

    Cel. Was't you, that did so oft contrive to kill him?

    Oli. 'Twas I; but 'tis not I: I do not shame
To tell you what I was, since my conversion
So sweetly tastes, being the thing I am.

    Ros. But, for the bloody napkin?—

    Oli. By and by.
When from the first to last, betwixt us two,
Tears our recountments had most kindly bath'd,
As, how I came into that desert place;——

In brief, he led me to the gentle duke,
Who gave me fresh array, and entertainment,
Committing me unto my brother's love;
Who led me instantly into his cave,
There stripp'd himself, and here upon his arm
The lioness had torn some flesh away,
Which all this while had bled; and now he fainted,
And cry'd, in fainting, upon Rosalind.
Brief, I recover'd him; bound up his wound;
And, after some small space, being strong at heart,
He sent me hither, stranger as I am,
To tell this story, that you might excuse
His broken promise, and to give this napkin,
Dy'd in this blood, unto the shepherd youth,
That he in sport doth call his Rosalind.

Cel. Why, how now, Ganymede? sweet Ganymede?

[~~ROSALIND faints.~~

Oli. Many will swoon when they do look on blood.

Cel. There is more in it:—Cousin—Ganymede!

Oli. Look, he recovers.

Ros. I would, I were at home.

Cel. We'll lead you thither:—
I pray you, will you take him by the arm?

Oli. Be of good cheer, youth:—You a man?—
You lack a man's heart.

Ros. I do so, I confess it. Ah, sir, a body would think this was well counterfeited: I pray you, tell your brother how well I counterfeited.—Heigh ho!—

Oli. This was not counterfeit; there is too great testimony in your complexion, that it was a passion of earnest.

Ros. Counterfeit, I assure you.

Q / Ros' faints - as she is falling backwards - she is caught by Gtis'
and Bel' /

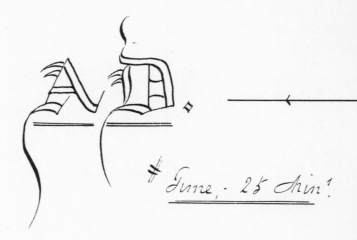

THE PLAYING TIME OF ACT IV. This, the shortest act (425 lines cut to 365), played rather slowly (under fifteen lines per minute) in about twenty-five minutes. Willmott noted its ending variously at "25 p 9," "28 p 9," and "33 p 9."

Oli. Well then, take a good heart, and counterfeit
to be a man.

Ros. So I do: but, i'faith I should have been a woman by right.

Cel. Come, you look paler and paler; pray you,
draw homewards:—Good sir, go with us.

Oli. That will I, for I must bear answer back
How you excuse my brother, Rosalind.

Ros. I shall devise something: But, I pray you,
commend my counterfeiting to him:—Will you go?

[*Exeunt, L.*]

ACT V.

SCENE I.—*The same.* / *Before the cottage.* /

Enter TOUCHSTONE *and* AUDREY. *L.*

Touch. We shall find a time, Audrey; patience, gentle Audrey.

Aud. 'Faith, the priest was good enough, for all the old gentleman's saying.

Touch. A most wicked sir Oliver, Audrey, a most vile Mar-text. But, Audrey, there is a youth here in the forest lays claim to you.

Aud. Ay, I know who 'tis; he hath no interest in me in the world: here comes the man you mean.

Enter WILLIAM, *L.*

Touch. It is meat and drink to me to see a clown: By my troth, we, that have good wits, have much to answer for; we shall be flouting; we cannot hold.

Will. Good even, Audrey.

Aud. ~~God~~ ^give ye good even, William.

Will. And good even to you, sir.

Touch. Good even, gentle friend: Cover thy head, cover thy head; nay, pr'ythee, be covered. How old are you, friend?

Will. Five and twenty, sir.

Touch. A ripe age: Is thy name, William?

5

THE STAGING OF V. 1 (Folio, V. 1, 2, and 3) (243 lines cut to 219). The act drop rose on the cottage scene, set in the second grooves and the second entrance right, as in III. 3 and IV. 1.

/ 2 gro^s. /

1.-

Touchstone.
Audrey.
William.
Corin.

2.-

Oliver
Orlando.
    Sling Bandage.
Rosalind.

Ø / <u>William retreats - in fright and bewilderment - round the stage,
before Gouch,' - And 'remaining C, - quietly enjoying William's
distress.</u> /

Will. William, sir.

Touch. A fair name: Wast born i'the forest here?

Will. Ay, sir, I thank ~~God~~. *Heaven.*

Touch. Thank ~~God~~; *Heaven;*—a good answer: Art rich?

Will. 'Faith, sir, so, so.

Touch. *So, so,* is good, very good, very excellent good:—and yet it is not; it is but so so. Art thou wise?

Will. Ay, sir, I have a pretty wit.

Touch. Why, thou say'st well. I do now remember a saying; *The fool doth think he is wise, but the wise man knows himself to be a fool.* The heathen philosopher, when he had a desire to eat a grape, would open his lips when he put it into his mouth; meaning thereby, that grapes were made to eat, and lips to open. You do love this maid?

Will. I do, sir.

Touch. Give me your hand: Art thou learned?

Will. No, sir.

Touch. Then learn this of me; To have, is to have: For it is a figure in rhetorick, that drink, being poured out of a cup into a glass, by filling the one doth empty the other: For all your writers do consent, that *ipse* is he; now you are not *ipse*, for I am he.

Will. Which he, sir?

Touch. He, sir, that must marry this woman: Therefore, you clown, abandon,—which is in the vulgar, leave,—the society,—which in the boorish is, company,—of this female,—which in the common is,— woman, which together is, abandon the society of this female; or, clown, thou perishest; or, to thy better understanding, diest; to wit, I kill thee, make thee away, translate thy life into death, thy liberty into bondage: I will deal in poison with thee, or in bastinado, or in steel; I will bandy with thee in faction; I will o'er-run thee with policy; I will kill thee a hundred and fifty ways; therefore tremble, and depart.

Aud. Do, good William.

Will. ~~God~~Rest you merry, sir.   [*Exit,* *L.*

Enter CORIN, *R. 2 E.*

Cor. Our master and mistress seek you; come, away, away.

Touch. Trip, Audrey, trip, Audrey;—I attend, I attend.   [*Exeunt.*

R. 2 E.]

~~SCENE II.—*The same*~~.

2.-   1.-

Enter ORLANDO *and* OLIVER. *L.*

Orl. Is't possible, that on so little acquaintance you should like her? that, but seeing, you should love her? and, loving, woo? and, wooing, she should grant? and will you perséver to enjoy her?

Oli. Neither call the giddiness of it in question, the poverty of her, the small acquaintance, my sudden wooing, nor her sudden consenting; but say with me, I love Aliena; say with her, that she loves me; consent with both, that we may enjoy each other: it shall be to your good; for my father's house, and all the revenue that was old sir Rowland's, will I estate upon you, and here live and die a shepherd.

3.-

Silvius
phoebe

Enter ROSALIND. *R-2E.-*

Orl. You have my consent. Let your wedding be to-morrow: thither will I invite the duke, and all his contented followers: Go you, and prepare Aliena; for, look you, here comes my Rosalind.

Ros. ~~God~~ save you, brother.

in Heaven

Oli. And you, fair sister. */Exit, R-2E.-/*

Ros. O, my dear Orlando, how it grieves me to see thee wear thy heart in a scarf.

Orl. It is my arm.

Ros. I thought, thy heart had been wounded with the claws of a lion.

Orl. Wounded it is, but with the eyes of a lady.

Ros. Did your brother tell you how I counterfeited to swoon, when he showed me your handkerchief?

Orl. Ay, and greater wonders than that.

Ros. O, I know where you are:—Nay, 'tis true: there was never any thing so sudden, but the fight of two rams, and Cæsar's thrasonical brag of—*I came, saw,* and *overcame:* For your brother and my sister no sooner met, but they looked; no sooner looked, but they loved; no sooner loved, but they sighed; no sooner sighed, but they asked one another the reason; no sooner knew the reason, but they sought the reme-dy: and in these degrees have they made a pair of stairs to marriage, ~~which they will climb incontinent, or else be incontinent before marriage:~~ they are in the very wrath of love, and they will together; clubs can-not part them.

they are in the

Orl. They shall be married to-morrow; and I will bid the duke to the nuptial. But, O, how bitter a thing it is to look into happiness through another man's eyes! By so much the more shall I to-morrow be at the height of heart-heaviness, by how much I shall think my brother happy, in having what he wishes for.

Ros. Why then, to-morrow I cannot serve your turn for Rosalind?

Orl. I can live no longer by thinking.

Ros. I will weary you no longer then with idle talking. Know of me then, (for now I speak to some purpose,) that I know you are a gentleman of good conceit: I speak not this, that you should bear a good opinion of my knowledge, insomuch, I say, I know you are; neither do I labour for a greater esteem than may in some little measure draw a belief from you, to do yourself good, and not to grace me. Believe then, if you please, that I can do strange things: I have, since I was three years old, conversed with a magician, most profound in this art, and yet not damnable. If you do love Rosalind so near the heart as your gesture cries it out, when your brother marries Aliena, shall you marry her: I know into what straits of fortune she is driven; and it is not impossible to me, if it appear not inconvenient to you, to set her before your eyes to-morrow, human as she is, and without any danger.

Orl. Speakest thou in sober meanings?

Ros. By my life, I do; which I tender dearly, though I say I am a magician: Therefore, put you in your best array, bid your friends; for if you will be married to-morrow, you shall; and to Rosalind, if you will.

4⁰

Touchstone.
Audrey.   } /Act./
1st & 2nd /pages.
      /Lutes./
3 Foresters.

RESTORATION. Macready restored Silvius' speech on the nature of love and most of the antiphonal howling of the cross-purposed lovers. The roughly scribbled cut is evidently Vezin's.

2.-   /.-

Enter Silvius, *and* Phebe. *L.-*

Look, here comes a lover of mine, and a lover of hers.o

 Phe. Youth, you have done me much ungentleness,
To show the letter that I writ to you.

 Ros. I care not, if I have; it is my study,
To seem despiteful and ungentle to you:
You are there follow'd by a faithful shepherd;
Look upon him, love him; he worships you.

 Phe. Good shepherd, tell this youth what 'tis to
   love.

 Sil. It is to be all made of sighs and tears;— */X L C.-/*
And so am I for Phebe.

L.- *Phe.* And I for Ganymede.

 Orl. And I for Rosalind.

RC *Ros.* And I for no woman.

 Sil. It is to be all made of faith and service;—
And so am I for Phebe.

 Phe. And I for Ganymede.

R.- *Orl.* And I for Rosalind.

 Ros. And I for no woman.

 Sil. It is to be all made of fantasy,
All made of passion, and all made of wishes;
All adoration, duty and observance,
All humbleness, all patience, and impatience,
All purity, all trial, all observance;—
And so am I for Phebe.

 Phe. And so am I for Ganymede.

 Orl. And so am I for Rosalind.

 Ros. And so am I for no woman.

 Phe. If this be so, why blame you me to love you?
         [To Rosalind.

Sil. If this be so, why blame you me to love you?
                          [*To* PHEBE.

Orl. If this be so, why blame you me to love you?

Ros. Who do you speak to, *why blame you me to love you?*

Orl. To her, that is not here, nor doth not hear.

Ros. Pray you, no more of this; 'tis like the howling of Irish wolves against the moon.—I will help you, [*To* SILVIUS] if I can :—I would love you, [*To* PHEBE] if I could.—To-morrow meet me all together.—I will marry you, [*To* PHEBE] if ever I marry woman, and I'll be married to-morrow :—I will satisfy you, [*To* ORLANDO] if ever I satisfied man, and you shall be married to-morrow :—I will content you, [*To* SILVIUS] if what pleases you contents you, and you shall be married to-morrow.—As you, [*To* ORLANDO] love Rosalind, meet ;—as you, [*To* SILVIUS] love Phebe, meet ; And as I love no woman, I'll meet.—So, fare you well ; I have left you commands. ——— *[Exit. R-2 C.]*

Sil. I'll not fail, if I live.

Phe. Nor I.

Orl. Nor I.
                                [*Exeunt. L.*

SCENE III.—*The same.*

Enter TOUCHSTONE *and* AUDREY. *R-2 C.*

Touch. To-morrow is the joyful day, Audrey, to-morrow will we be married.

Aud. I do desire it with all my heart : and I hope it is no dishonest desire, to desire to be a woman of

3

RESTORATION. Macready restored the scene and song of "It was a lover and his lass." The line introducing the song had to be tinkered to alter the song from a duet to a quintette.

⊘ |*All sit, &.-*|

5.-

Duke, Sen.ˢ
Amiens.
Jaques.
Orlando.
Oliver.
Celia.
Rosalind.
Silvius.
phœbe.
1ˢᵗ 2ⁿᵈ & 3ʳᵈ & Lords.
All the other D.ᵒ -
Hunters, - & Attend.ᵗˢ

for
end
of
piece

the world.   Here comes two of the banished duke's pages.

Enter two Pages. /with lute/ /-3 Foresters, R.-

1 *Page.* Well met, honest gentleman.

Touch. By my troth, well met : Come, sit, sit, and a song.

2 *Page.* We are for you : sit i'the middle. ⊗

[Miss Reeves
Stretton
Clifford]

1 *Page.* Shall we clap into't roundly, without hawking, or spitting, or saying we are hoarse ; which are the only prologues to a bad voice ?

2 *Page.* I'faith, i'faith ; and ~~both~~ all in a tune, ~~like two gypsies on a horse.~~

~~SONG.~~ Quintette

𝄢 5.-

I.

It was a lover, and his lass,
  With a hey, and a ho, and a hey nonino,
That o'er the green corn-field did pass
  In the spring time, the only pretty rank time,
When birds do sing, hey ding a ding, ding ;
Sweet lovers love the spring.

II.

Between the acres of the rye,
  With a hey, and a ho, and a hey nonino,
These pretty country folks would lie,
  In spring time, &c.

III.

This carol they began that hour,
　With a hey, and a ho, and a hey nonino,
How that a life was but a flower
　In spring time, &c.

II.

And therefore take the present time,
　With a hey, and a ho, and a hey nonino ;
For love is crowned with the prime
　In spring time, &c.　　　　　　　　　*/All rue./*

Touch. Truly, young gentlemen, though there was
no greater matter in the ditty, yet the note was very
untuneable.

　1 Page. You are deceived, sir; we kept time, we
lost not our time.

　Touch. By my troth, yes; I count it but time lost to
\Heaven hear such a foolish song ⋀ ~~God~~ be with you ; and ~~God~~ *Heaven*
mend your voices! Come, Audrey.　　　　*[Exeunt.*

2ᵈ

SCENE ~~IV.~~ —*Another part of the Forest. - The Beechen*

Enter Duke senior, AMIENS, JAQUES, ORLANDO,
　　　　　　OLIVER, *and* CELIA. *All the Forest Lords —*

Duke S. Dost thou believe, Orlando, that the boy
Can do all this that he hath promised?

　Orl. I sometimes do believe, and sometimes do not ;
As those that fear they hope, and know they fear.

——————————————⟶ ——— *pages & Foresters follow, repeating the burthen, "When birds do sing, &c -L-*

Avenue".(-An entire set of the whole stage.)

- Foresters - Attendants, &c altogether, from R-ll Ent.

THE STAGING OF V. 2. (Folio, V. 4) (226 lines cut to 218). The cottage and its
flats drew off to reveal "The Beechen Avenue"—"An entire set of the whole stage."
This probably means again, as in I. 2, that a vast drop-scene was hung at the back
of the stage, this time representing a perspective avenue of beech trees, with matching
wood-wings set in the grooves.

$\overline{\underline{6.}}$

Hymen. /The "1st page". /

All the Shepherds

and

Shepherdesses.

Baskets - and - Garlands
of Flowers, - Poles, - &c -
for Temple.

b.-

Enter ROSALIND, SILVIUS, *and* PHEBE. *L-llb.-*

Ros. Patience once more, whiles our compáct is
        urg'd :——
You say, if I bring in your Rosalind,

                        [*To the Duke.*

You will bestow her on Orlando here?
    Duke S. That would I, had I kingdoms to give with *b.-*
        her.
    Ros. And you say, you will have her, when I bring
        her?   [*To* ORLANDO.
    Orl. That would I, were I of all kingdoms king. - *R.-*
    Ros. You say, you'll marry me, if I be willing?

                        [*To* PHEBE.

    Phe. That will I, should I die the hour after.   - *L.-*
    Ros. But, if you do refuse to marry me,
You'll give yourself to this most faithful shepherd?
    Phe. So is the bargain.
    Ros. You say, that you'll have Phebe, if she will?

                        [*To* SILVIUS.

    Sil. Though to have her and death were both one *L.-*
        thing.
    Ros. I have promis'd to make all this matter even.
Keep you your word, O duke, to give your daughter;—
You yours, Orlando, to receive his daughter:—
Keep your word, Phebe, that you'll marry me;
Or else, refusing me, to wed this shepherd:—
Keep your word, Silvius, that you'll marry her,
If she refuse me :—and from hence I go,
To make these doubts all even.
                [*Exeunt* ROSALIND *and* CELIA. *L,-llb.-*

Duke S. I do remember in this shepherd-boy
Some lively touches of my daughter's favour.

   Orl. My lord, the first time, that I ever saw him,
Methought he was a brother to your daughter:
But, my good lord, this boy is forest-born;
And hath been tutor'd in the rudiments
Of many desperate studies by his uncle,
Whom he reports to be a great magician,
Obscured in the circle of this forest.

     Enter TOUCHSTONE *and* AUDREY. *L-21 C.-*

   R.- *Jaq.* There is, sure, another flood toward, and these
couples are coming to the ark! Here comes a pair of
very strange beasts, which in all tongues are called
fools.

   L.- *Touch.* Salutation and greeting to you all!

   Jaq. Good my lord, bid him welcome; This is the
motley-minded gentleman, that I have so often met in
the forest: he hath been a courtier, he swears.

   Touch. If any man doubt that, let him put me to my
purgation. I have trod a measure; I have flattered a
lady; I have been politick with my friend, smooth with
mine enemy; I have undone three tailors; I have had
four quarrels, and like to have fought one.

   Jaq. And how was that ta'en up?

   Touch. 'Faith, we met, and found the quarrel was
upon the seventh cause.

   Jaq. How seventh cause?—Good my lord, like this
fellow.

   Duke S. I like him very well.

   Heaven   *Touch.* ~~God~~'ild you, sir; I desire you of the like. I
press in here, sir, amongst the rest of the country co-

Ø Touch' / with^t L. U C. - / Come along, Audrey.

pulatives, to swear, and to forswear; according as marriage binds, and blood breaks:—A poor virgin, sir, an
ill-favoured thing, sir, but mine own; a poor humour
of mine, sir, to take that, that no man else will: Rich
honesty dwells like a miser, sir, in a poor-house; as
your pearl, in your foul oyster.

Duke S. By my faith, he is very swift and senten-
tious.

Touch. According to the fool's bolt, sir, and such
dulcet diseases.

Jaq. But, for the seventh cause: how did you find
the quarrel on the seventh cause?

Touch. Upon a lie seven times removed;—Bear your
body more seeming, Audrey:—as thus, sir.   I did dis-
like the cut of a certain courtier's beard; he sent me
word, if I said his beard was not cut well, he was in the
mind it was: This is called the *Retort courteous.*   If I
sent him word again, it was not well cut, he would send
me word, he cut it to please himself: This is called the
Quip modest.   If again, it was not well cut, he disabled
my judgment: This is call'd the *Reply churlish.*   If
again, it was not well cut, he would answer, I spake not
true: This is call'd the *Reproof valiant.*   If again, it
was not well cut, he would say, I lie: This is called the
Countercheck quarrelsome: and so to the *Lie circumstan-
tial,* and the *Lie direct.*

Jaq. And how oft did you say, his beard was not
well cut?

Touch. I durst go no further than the *Lie circumstan-
tial,* nor he durst not give me the *Lie direct;* and so we
measured swords, and parted.

Jaq. Can you nominate in order now the degrees of the lie?

Touch. O sir, we quarrel in print, by the book; as you have books for good manners: I will name you the degrees. The first, the Retort courteous; the second, the Quip modest; the third, the Reply churlish; the fourth, the Reproof valiant; the fifth, the Countercheck quarrelsome; the sixth, the Lie with circumstance; the seventh, the Lie direct. All these you may avoid, but the lie direct; and you may avoid that too, with an *If.* I knew when seven justices could not take up a quarrel; but when the parties were met themselves, one of them thought but of an *If,* as, *If you said so, then I said so;* and they shook hands, and swore brothers. Your *If* is the only peace-maker: much virtue in *If.*

Jaq. Is not this a rare fellow, my lord? he's as good at any thing, and yet a fool.

Duke S. He uses his folly like a stalking-horse, and under the presentation of that, he shoots his wit. ○———

~~Enter HYMEN, leading ROSALIND in woman's clothes,~~
and CELIA.

Still Musick.

Hym. *Then is there mirth in heaven,*
      When earthly things made even
      Atone together.

Song — Hym. *Good duke, receive thy daughter,*
      Hymen from heaven brought her,
           Yea, brought her hither;
      That thou might'st join her hand with his,
      Whose heart within her bosom is.

/At end of Song, — Hymen leads Rosal¹- as she enters, L·2·E,—
with Celia, and Six Shepherdesses, — to L· of Duke./

RESTORATION. Only a token few lines of the Hymen scene had traditionally been spoken or sung. Macready made an elaborate masque of it: Helen Faucit remembered it long afterwards as too long but "beautiful . . . in itself, and bringing this charming love-romance most appropriately to a close" (*Some of Shakespeare's Female Characters,* p. 280). A prize of £10 was awarded Mr. Henry Smart, nephew of the eminent conductor Sir George Smart, for his music to Hymen's song.

Music. - A crowd of Shepherds and Shepherdesses, enter L-UE.- with poles,-garlands & baskets of flowers, - dancing - and as they dance, erect a kind of rural temple, in C,- at back,- and place an altar within it, to which, they conduct one of the pages - attired as -"Hymen;- at the first sound of the music, all the Characters, in front, divide R & L,- and come down the stage.

Song. - / Hymen. /
~~Then is there mirth~~ &c / omitted. /
Good duke, receive &c

Ros. To you I give myself, for I am yours.

[*To Duke S.*

To you I give myself, for I am yours.   [*To* ORLANDO.

Duke S. If there be truth in sight, you are my daughter.

Orl. If there be truth in sight, you are my Rosalind.

Phe. If sight and shape be true,
Why then,—my love-adieu!

Ros. I'll have no father, if you be not he :—

[*To Duke S.*

I'll have no husband, if you be not he :—

[*To* ORLANDO.

Nor ne'er wed woman, if you be not she.

(*adv J.*)   [*To* PHEBE.

Hym. Peace, ho! I bar confusion :
    ^"Tis I must make conclusion
        Of these most strange events :
        Here's eight that must take hands,
        To join in Hymen's bands,
            If truth holds true contents.
    You and you no cross shall part :

[*To* ORLANDO *and* ROSALIND. *R C.-*)

    You and you are heart in heart :

L C.-   [*To* OLIVER *and* CELIA. *L C.-*)

    You [*To* PHEBE] to his love must accord,
    Or have a woman to your lord :—
    You and you are sure together,

[*To* TOUCHSTONE *and* AUDREY. *L.-*)

    As the winter to foul weather.
    Whiles a wedlock-hymn we sing,
    Feed yourselves with questioning ;

That reason wonder may diminish,
How thus we met, and these things finish.

Chorus. ~~Song.~~

Wedding is great Juno's crown;
    O blessed bond of board and bed!
'Tis Hymen peoples every town;
    High wedlock then be honoured:
Honour, high honour, and renown,
To Hymen, god of every town!

Duke S. O my dear niece, welcome thou art to me;
Even daughter, welcome in no less degree.

~~*Phe.* I will not eat my word, now thou art mine;~~
~~Thy faith my fancy to thee doth combine.~~

                                    [*To* ~~Silvius.~~

Enter JAQUES DE BOIS. *L.*

Jaq. de B. Let me have audience for a word, or two;
I am the second son of old sir Rowland,
That bring these tidings to this fair assembly :—
Duke Frederick, hearing how that every day
Men of great worth resorted to this forest,
Address'd a mighty power; which were on foot,
In his own conduct, purposely to take
His brother here, and put him to the sword :
And to the skirts of this wild wood he came;
Where, meeting with an old religious man,
After some question with him, was converted
Both from his enterprize, and from the world :
His crown bequeathing to his banish'd brother,
And all their lands restor'd to them again

7.

Jaques de Bois.

(Towards the end of this, Touch' and Aud' go up.)

Q /Jaques de Bois X'es over to his brothers, - Touch' and Aud'
X beh^d to R.- /

/X'g to L- / -

⊙ /Touch' & Aud' come down R,- when Jaques addresses them. /

That were with him exíl'd : This to be true,
I do engage my life.

    Duke S. Welcome, young man ;
Thou offer'st fairly to thy brother's wedding :
~~To one, his lands withheld ; and to the other,~~
~~A land itself at large, a potent dukedom.~~
First, in this forest, let us do those ends,
That here were well begun, and well begot :
And after, every of this happy number,
That have endur'd shrewd days and nights with us,
Shall share the good of our returned fortune,
According to the measure of their states.
Meantime, forget this new-fall'n dignity,
And fall into our rustick revelry :—
Play, musick ;—and you brides and bridegrooms all,
With measure heap'd in joy, to the measures fall.

    Jaq. Sir, by your patience ; If I heard you rightly,
The duke hath put on a religious life,
And thrown into neglect the pompous court?

    Jaq de B. He hath.

    Jaq. To him will I : out of these convertites
There is much matter to be heard and learn'd.—
You to your former honour I bequeath ;

                           [*To Duke S.*
Your patience, and your virtue, well deserves it :—
You [*To* ORLANDO] to a love, that your true faith doth
           merit :—
You [*To* OLIVER] to your land, and love, and great al-
           lies :—
You [*To* SILVIUS] to a long and well deserved bed ;—
And you [*To* TOUCHSTONE] to wrangling ; for thy lov-
           ing voyage

Is but for two months victual'd :—So to your pleasures;
I am for other than for dancing measures.

 Duke S. Stay, Jaques, stay.

 Jaq. To see no pastime, I :—what you would have
I'll stay to know at your abandon'd cave.   [*Exit, L.-]*

 Duke S. Proceed, proceed: we will begin these rites,
And we do trust they'll end, in true delights.

             [*A Dance.*

EPILOGUE.

 Ros. It is not the fashion to see the lady the epilogue; but it is no more unhandsome, than to see the lord the prologue. If it be true, that *good wine needs no bush,* 'tis true, that a good play needs no epilogue: Yet to good wine they do use good bushes; and good plays prove the better by the help of good epilogues. What a case am I in then, that am neither a good epilogue, nor cannot insinuate with you in the behalf of a good play? I am not furnished like a beggar, therefore to beg will not become me: my way is, to conjure you; and I'll begin with the women. I charge you, O women, for the love you bear to men, to like as much of this play as please them: and so I charge you, O men, for the love you bear to women, (as I perceive by your simpering, none of you hate them,) that between you and the women, the play may please. If I were a woman, I would kiss as many of you as had beards that

among you,